To: _____

From: _____

Date: _____

May the Secrets of the Pink House help you find
personal peace and professional success.

Secrets of the Pink House

FROM SALTWATER TO HOLY WATER

JACK MANILLA

WESTBOW
PRESS®
A DIVISION OF THOMAS NELSON
& ZONDERVAN

WestBow Press books may be ordered through booksellers or by contacting:

WestBow Press
A Division of Thomas Nelson & Zondervan
1663 Liberty Drive
Bloomington, IN 47403
www.westbowpress.com
1 (866) 928-1240

ISBN: 978-1-5127-9657-5 (sc)
ISBN: 978-1-5127-9659-9 (hc)
ISBN: 978-1-5127-9658-2 (e)

Library of Congress Control Number: 2017911210

Print information available on the last page.

WestBow Press rev. date: 8/2/2017

Dedication

To Paula,
For your amazing perseverance and love.
To our children,
Jackie, John, Paul, and Brad,
Your spouses and close friends,
Our grandchildren and great-grandchildren,
Our personal friends and associates,
All ministers, clergy, ordained men and women,
Remember God made us one family!
We need one another. We forgive one another.
We play together. We dine together.
We work together.

To the readers
"For this reason, I kneel before the Father, from whom every
family in heaven and on earth is named, that he may grant
you in accord with the riches of his glory to be strengthened
with power through his Spirit in the inner self, and that Christ
may dwell in your hearts through faith; that you, rooted and
grounded in love, may have strength to comprehend with all the
holy ones what is the breadth and length and height and depth,
and to know the love of Christ that surpasses knowledge, so
that you may be filled with all the fullness of God. Now to him
who is able to accomplish far more than all we ask or imagine,
by the power at work within us, to him be glory in the church
and in Christ Jesus to all generations, forever and ever. Amen."
(Ephesians 3:14–21)

CONTENTS

FOREWORD

I was awakened to Christ in my life some eighteen years ago when I attended my first Christ Renews His Parish renewal weekend. It also happened to be my very first encounter with Jack Manilla, who served as a member of the presenting team. Now to be clear, it wasn't that God hadn't provided me more than my fair share of opportunities to accept him as my personal savior, for He had always been a part of my life. But like so many others, I would only call upon Him in times of trial or periodically acknowledge the many blessings He afforded me throughout my life. It was the experience of that weekend where I began the rest of my journey with Christ *in* my life, and like Jack, I now share the table of plenty with Christ as my Lord and Savior.

During the course of my faith journey, in recent years I came to appreciate there was no such thing as coincidence, and such was the case here. As I read with great interest Jack's words (even though I was already familiar with many of the stories he shared), I kept coming back to what I would characterize as the unifying theme throughout—trust in the Lord. I honestly struggled with the idea of boiling the learning he shares and the encouragement he offers throughout to four simple words. "Would that be fair to him? Have I missed the larger lesson he was trying to impart? Did he err in asking me to write this foreword?"

My concerns were allayed a few days ago when I received a pamphlet and letter from the bishop of the Diocese of St. Augustine, the honorable Bishop Felipe J. Estevez, concerning the upcoming stewardship appeal campaign. There boldly emblazoned on the cover were those very four words, "Trust in the LORD" (Proverbs 3:5).

With that matter behind me, allow me to do a couple of things with the few paragraphs I can offer here. The first is to affirm Jack. We have been friends for these past eighteen years, and in many respects, he is my spiritual mentor. Ever since his first road trip to the monastery of the Holy Spirit, we have made that pilgrimage together for more than a dozen years. While it's never been easy for me to seek out a friend to lean on anyone for help, with Jack I never had to because he made it incredibly easy to do so. Oftentimes it would be a phone call out of the blue, a brief encounter after church or at a community event, or the time he joined me for that difficult journey to Ohio for the funeral of my sister, which he references in the pages of this book.

The second is to commend him for sharing his story and the lessons he imparts throughout. I suspect as you read about the many challenges he faced, those brought on by others, but by his own admission, the larger ones being self-inflicted, you may find it difficult to live up to or relate to them, given where you are in your relationship with Christ. Trust me. Jack is no different than any one of us. I have heard his witness many times over. In each instance, he talks about his weaknesses, his humanness, as he does here. Typically, his message would include this phrase, "We fall down. We get up." Jack knows too well that God joyfully meets all us wherever we may be in our faith journey. I know that it's his prayer, his words here, that will help you in yours.

And finally, I want to reflect on the very important message Jack is imparting with the words of Mother Teresa, "We are not called to be successful. We are called to be faithful." What a remarkable revelation, one that is found throughout all of the chapters of this book. Please don't mistake, however, that to mean success is an impedance to a powerful, personal relationship with Christ. God has blessed each of us with many gifts that can lead to prosperity. It would be a disservice to Him if we did not take full advantage of the opportunities He has afforded us. Jack learned that lesson the hard way. He viewed his earlier successes as his alone. It took being "stripped down" (as he calls it) for him to come to understand and appreciate that success and continued success, for that matter, is only possible with God as your counsel and partner. Realizing too, that to whom much is given, much is expected.

I applaud Jack for sharing his very personal life story and the lessons he learned along the way. I pray that you will learn much from reading this and that it helps you in your journey toward answering the call to be faithful.

—Michael Boylan

PREFACE

> Then he said, "Write these words down,
> for they are trustworthy and true."
> (Revelation 21:5)

My Lord God, I have no idea where I am going. I do not see the road ahead of me. I cannot know for certain where it will end. Nor do I really know myself, and the fact that I think that I am following your will does not mean that I am actually doing so. But I believe that the desire to please you does in fact please you. And I hope I have that desire in all that I am doing. I hope that I will never do anything apart from that desire. And I know that if I do this you will lead me by the right road though I may know nothing about it. Therefore, will I trust you always though I may seem to be lost and in the shadow of death. I will not fear, for you are ever with me, and you will never leave me to face my perils alone.
(Thomas Merton, *Thoughts in Solitude*)

Thomas Merton, OCSO (January 31, 1915—December 10, 1968), was an American Catholic writer and mystic. A Trappist monk of the Abbey of Gethsemanei, Kentucky, he was a poet, social activist, and student of comparative religion. In 1949, he was ordained to the priesthood and given the name Father Louis. Merton wrote more than seventy books, mostly on spirituality, social justice and a quiet pacifism, as well as scores of essays and reviews

The psalmist wrote, "The steps of a good man are ordered by the Lord, and He delights in his way" (Psalm 37:23). The passage continues with a loving description of God's faithful care for everyone who wants to walk with Him. "The law of his God is in his heart; none of his steps shall slide" (Psalm 37:31).

My writings are inspired by *Listening Prayers* as taught by the monks at the Retreat House of Our Lady of the Monastery of the Holy Spirit, Conyers, Georgia. Special recognition is extended to Father Anthony Delisi, OCSO monk and priest (deceased), Fathers Tom Francis and Gerard, and Brother Michael, who teach how to listen using the monk's daily prayer, *Lectio Divina* (Divine Reading). The monk's prayer fills the inner desire of the heart, one drop at a time.

Linda Mitchell, spiritual director, Father Anthony Delisi, and Father Tom Francis provided personal spiritual direction and encouragement to me during annual retreats to the monastery. Reverend Edward Booth, a former pastor, provided spiritual and practical guidance to my wife Paula and me at our local church. Reverend John Tetlow, current pastor, modeled *The Lessons* in his easily understood, practical application of scriptural passages to everyday living during his Sunday homilies.

Unless otherwise noted that other Bible Translations were used, Bible Translations are from the *New American Bible, revised edition* © (updated 2011) *2010*, 1991, 1986, 1970 Confraternity of Christian Doctrine, Inc. reviewed and approved by The United States Conference of Catholic Bishops.

Practicing Lectio Divina, I recorded my reflective thoughts in a daily journal for more than ten years. These journal entries formed the spiritual core of the book. *The Secrets* were discovered and then woven within his personal life experience. Stories led to learning of *The Lessons*: stories from my childhood, adolescence, and adulthood to years of dramatic storms on the saltwater sea of life that brought me to change self, to transform materially, mentally, and spiritually.

Lectio Divina is a four-step process. It includes short scripture reading, meditation, personal prayer to God from the heart, and contemplation. Perhaps it is best explained as abiding in restful calm, in company with God without thoughts, words, or images. This contrasts with the many forms of beautiful, wonderful, common childhood *talking prayers* that most are familiar with.

Each of us could create a record of God's leading and faithfulness, reflecting on God's guidance—the people, places, and experiences that are landmarks on our pathway of faith through life. Every remembrance of the Lord's goodness encourages us to keep walking with Him and to thank someone who influenced us for good.

I started journaling soon after my first visit to the monastery and draw from these journals in presenting my stories to business executives with the goal of leading others to Jesus Christ and to integrate their spiritual beliefs into the workplace. The Lord comes first. The benefit: personal peace and a balanced life.

Secrets of the Pink House is my story of seventy-six years of growth in grace and awareness that led me to a personal relationship with my Lord Jesus Christ. Key people and dramatic events are spaced between years of ordinary everyday living in my journey of faith over nearly eight decades.

What seemed to be normal, practical choices at the time— morning newspaper carrier, altar server, college, career pursuit, religion instructor, ministry leader, meeting for prayer with others for others, telling fellow workers and parishioners about Jesus, critical ethical business decisions, loss of jobs—all became major turning points that changed the direction of my life. It has been fascinating and humbling to reflect on how God's hand guided and encouraged me through my struggles.

During my forty-year corporate career, I learned the ways of the privileged in today's times, acquiring many of their trappings. But I was always thirsting for something more, unable to understand or define what it was. Then I discovered I was sailing on a saltwater sea of life and realized my thirst might never be quenched.

It took a great storm of life to shipwreck me and bring me to this awareness. I lost everything earthly, fell into a great pit of desperation, and found everything spiritually when I surrendered my will to the Lord.

He then rescued me and brought me to the *Pink House* in the middle of a Florida orange grove. There, He quenched my thirst and I found rest, joy, and peace. The scriptures call it a "spring of (holy) water welling up to eternal life" (John 4:14).

At the *Pink House,* a remarkable conversation with God began as He prepared me for a new life, a personal spiritual Exodus, much like that which Moses led. Moses lived forty years in Pharaoh's palace, learning the ways of the privileged Egyptians. Moses also lived another forty years in the desert learning humility and the ways of commoners. This prepared him for service to our Lord, to lead his people to Him.

During the 18 months, I lived in the *Pink House*, I gained clarity of thought, a realization, an insight, perspective, and new understanding that each of us will someday go out from this earthly world to eternity—our personal exodus. In the time we have left, we each have a choice to ignore it and do nothing or to heed it and do something to prepare for the journey. We can pursue the ways of the world and be eternally lost in the desert or choose the path to God and exodus to His Promised Land.

Like Moses I went through several stages, from the no to anger to humility. I literally spoke my thoughts and feelings aloud, shouting to God in the clouds above, raising my fist as I walked through an orange grove several times each day. When I finally emptied it all, calmed down, stopped talking, and began to listen, I was given a special gift that led me to new insights to the words of the Lord—His secrets. I later learned a term defining this gift—*enlightenment.*

"Then he opened their minds to understand the scriptures."
(Luke 24:45)

God is timeless. The scriptures are timeless. They are messages from God, and they come with personal encouragement, reprimand, guidance, and challenges. They speak clearly to those who seek to understand them. Today their depth of meaning is the same as when they were first recorded thousands of years ago.

Several times a day, I returned to the *Pink House* from my walks in the orange grove with an increasing thirst.

"Let anyone who thirsts come to me and drink."
(John 7:37)

This thirst was a spiritual thirst. A craving not known before. It was a desire for fellowship with God. He led me to read the Bible from cover to cover three times, first as a book on the history of mankind searching for personal purpose, second as a how-to book on successful living, and third as a book of conversation with God. I once heard someone describe the meaning of the letters spelling the word *Bible.*

The Secret: The meaning of the letters spelling the word Bible –

Basic Information Before Leaving Earth

The Lesson: The Bible is God's "Policy, Procedure, and Operations Manual."

Read, listen, learn, and do. HUA! ("Hoo-ah": Heard, Understood, Acknowledged)

Learning to truly listen has always been a struggle for me. While at the *Pink House*, I came to discover, as I spoke less and less and listened more and more, that my inner thirst was being quenched by the holy water of God's Word.

You too can drink from this well of holy water. It is located in a meadow behind the door of surrender next to a spiritual spiral. Upward advancement on the ramp is made through prayer, scripture meditation, and contemplation. Like most classroom learning, knowledge within the Bible is best understood when put into practice, hands-on in service to others. So, return to the well in the meadow daily and hydrate your mind, heart, and soul for the day's journey.

Remember: it is not what you say, but what you do that is remembered. History records for the most part what people have done. You and I are called to do service for the Lord. Service to others is service to God, and when we serve, we help others quench their spiritual thirsts by giving them cups of refreshing holy water.

> "Whoever drinks the water I shall give will never
> thirst; the water I shall give will become in him a
> spring of water welling up to eternal life."
> (John 4:14)

Secrets of The Pink House and the lessons that I share are my humble attempt to help people attain personal peace through God's saving grace. The lessons in the following pages are intended to empower you to find your own personal peace by surrendering and accepting God's will. He will help you. You only need to say yes.

The journey to personal peace, from saltwater to holy water, starts with surrendering control of your life and surrendering your will to God. The Lord protects, guides, and guards all who walk with Him.

Hubris, the opposite of humility, is a disease that will blind you and lead to loss of contact with reality and an overestimation of one's own competence, accomplishments, or capabilities, especially if you are in a position of power. The cure, personal surrender, is simple to say yet extremely difficult to do.

One of the greatest decisions you can make in life is yielding your will to God, suppressing ego, lowering pride, and truly becoming humble. For many, it takes going through the school of hard knocks and repeated storms of life to drive us onto the rocks and shipwreck before we become aware of this and totally surrender to God's will.

> "You have to get to a place where you scare yourself
> before you can better yourself."
> (Martin Luther)

This surrender is not one of shame and punishment, but one of welcoming joy and abundance. Know this: surrender is the key to the door of grace—supernatural power, strength, illumination, enlightenment, and divine revelation.

When difficulties occur recall the darkest and most difficult time in your life and be grateful that you are better off now than you were then. For me, when difficulties come, and they do quite often, I recall my great personal storm, shipwreck, and landing on the rocks at Safety Harbor, Florida. I was then led to the Pink House in an orange grove and found a well fed by the spring of holy water.

Secrets of the Pink House: From Saltwater to Holy Water is my story and the lessons are those that I learned, taught by scripture reading and experiences during years sailing the "saltwater sea of life," searching for my life's purpose and personal peace. My hope is you will come to a safe harbor and also find this well fed by the spring of holy water. Next to it is the spiritual ramp, the entrance behind the door of surrender. Your thirst will be quenched, and you'll find rest, joy, and peace.

"I have told you this so that you might have peace in me.

In the world you will have trouble, but take
courage, I have conquered the world."
(John 16:33)

Reflections on *The Secrets* and *The Lessons* are drawn
from my personal life experience, hopefully powerful,
practical and graceful. My transformation has been an
arduous lifelong struggle, involving periods of peace
and suffering through the storms of life, shipwrecks,
and washing ashore—*from saltwater to holy water.*
"The Lord promises peace, but not leisure, heart-
rest and comfort, but not pleasure."
(A. J. Russell, *God Calling*)

*Come, amazing adventures are waiting to be
discovered on the Sea of Life. Let's sail!*

ACKNOWLEDGMENTS

"A friend is a friend at all time."
(Proverbs 17:17)

I am extremely grateful to the many people who encouraged me to write Secrets of the Pink House. I thank everyone who patiently listened as I repeated the Pink House stories over and over to others. I would like to especially thank Jim Molis, writer consultant, for his perseverance and generous sharing of his talent and counsel.

I thank my wife, Paula, a loving, rare and remarkably great woman who has stood strong, behind and beside me, helping with the wheel during heavy storms on the sea of life.

I thank the monks of the Monastery of the Holy Spirit, Conyers, Georgia, especially Father Anthony Delisi, OCSO monk and priest; Fathers Tom Francis and Gerard; and Brother Michael, who inspired me to write. I thank the archangels: Michael, Gabriel, and Raphael, and my guardian angel, Samuel. I thank both Paula's family and mine: our grandparents, our parents, our brothers, my sister Arlene, our children (Jackie, John, Paul, and Brad), our nephews, nieces, uncles, aunts, and cousins, and all their spouses and children. I thank each of you for your love and counsel from childhood to present. I love you, my family and friends!

I thank my lower school and college teachers, especially Youngstown State University, Dean of Williamson College of Business Administration, Professor Brown, teacher and mentor. I thank our close friends for standing by us: Lou & Lynda Andres,

Vicki Harris, Skip and Janice Suss, Michael and Susan Boylan; Anthony M. Butler Sr., the Founder E3 Business Group and its members.

I especially thank Don Girvan, who introduced us to Al Jackson, founder Al Jackson Pools, and his wife, Melva, who together opened the door to a new career for us in pool water. I thank all the employees, subcontractors. manufacturers and suppliers of Portofino Pool Services & Outdoor Living and Portofino Pool University for your good work down through the years.

I thank all the ordained clergy and laypeople who participated with me during our years of ministry service in the process of *Christ Renews His Parish* at San Juan Del Rio Catholic Church. I thank my many pastors for their counsel, as my business career took our family around the United States in fifteen household moves.

Most recently, I thank Reverend Edward Booth and his successor, Reverend John Tetlow, Deacon Jerry Turkowski, and Deacon Larry Geinosky for their personal spiritual counsel.

I thank the members of Legatus, members of John Beehner's Wise Counsel, North Florida Hotel & Lodging Association, Southside Business Men's Club, Jacksonville Regional Chamber of Commerce, and all the special committees we served together on.

I thank the members of The Association of Pool and Spa Professionals, Florida Swimming Pool Association, International Swimming Hall of Fame and Museum and The National Swimming Pool Foundation.

I sincerely thank Michael Boylan, president and CEO, WJCT Public Broadcasting, for being my close friend, Christ Renews His Parish brother, and annual road trip partner to the monastery, as well as for writing the foreword to this book.

I thank all those I have met down through the years. Each person has truly influenced the person I am today. Having shaken the hands of four United States of America (USA) Presidents and Vice Presidents, many senators, congressmen, judges, mayors, city councilmen, corporate VIPs, small-business owners, served with members on many boards of directors, -- and worked with the humblest, hardest-working everyday people in the world, I beg your forgiveness for not naming you individually. Rest assured you played a lead part in molding the person I have become. You are always with me—and were with me—in my mind and heart as I composed this book.

Thanks go to WestBow Press for diligently following up with me on my progress in completing the book for publishing. I thank the entire team for your high editorial standards, publishing expertise, and the personal freedom that enabled me to openly share my experiences and thoughts on paper and through digital print with the many people who read this book. I humbly say, thank you! And most importantly of all:

I love, thank and Praise God, the Father,
the Son, and the Holy Spirit.
Amen!

Do I Know Jack!

Jack and I have been dating for fifty-eight years and have been married now for fifty-seven. Together, we have raised four children and five grandchildren. We are excited as we now welcome our first great-grandchild into our family.

Though we have been together closely all of our adult lives, I was still very emotionally touched when I first read the manuscript. So many names, faces and memories returned: some fond, some good, some bad, all indelible.

Jack and I have been through so much together. We often felt as though the two of us were all alone during the tough times. Whether it was a financial hardship, parenting challenge, or a difficulty in our own relationship, we felt as if we must have been the only people who had ever had to endure such things and that we perhaps would be the last who did. Like us, you also may feel you are alone when storms arise in your life. Don't.

Looking back in this season of life and sharing our personal stories with friends and others has taught us that we all experience difficulties throughout our lives—some strikingly enormous, some much less so. Our culture suppresses sharing difficulties with others and encourages boastful acclamations. I find that balance in most all things is best. In reading this book, I hope you too will find timeless inspiration and personal confidence as you discover the Secrets and Lessons revealed.

As we approach living sixty years together, it's hard to fathom that Jack and I ever felt alone because we never were. From friends to relatives to fellow churchgoers, others were always there for us. Reach out—you will find that others and God are always there for you.

We are most thankful that we always had each other—and that God, Emmanuel, is with us. Together, we surmounted insurmountable challenges. We survived. No. We thrived.

- I hope that you will discover in this book new strengths and grow your faith to trust in God.
- I hope that you will stop doubting and start believing.
- I hope that you will believe that the best of life is now and always to come.
- I hope you will come to truly live in the present moments, not the past or the future.
- I hope you will simplify your life and focus on the things that really matter. The ordinary everyday things— fellowship with family, friends, and others.

In our life together, Jack and I have come to know each other better than we know ourselves. I read scripture every morning and follow as best I can what it says about spreading God's love. I delight in seeing how happy people get when you simply smile at them, or maybe say hello. I pray for many people daily. Jack and I share the practice of rising in the very early morning hours before dawn to be together, abiding with the Lord—reading short scripture verses, devotionals, forming personal reflections.

I don't relish being in the company of many people. I prefer to be a homebody. I enjoy more quiet, personal, one-on-one conversations with a few close friends and those I encounter daily at work (Yes! Jack and I still work full-time in our business) or the post office or the grocery store, people from all walks of life. I pause and listen closely to their concerns and do what I can to counsel them in the moment. Most often a simple smile is all that is needed.

Jack is my opposite. He thrives on being with people. It energizes him. He's so loving and caring that he always makes time for a person, organization, or cause. He's always supporting others. If you meet him, you will think he always knows just what to say and when to say it. Many people marvel at the amount of time he has committed to volunteer in service for so many organizations through the years.

He's much different at home. He's quiet, pensive. He doesn't discuss his feelings very often. But I always know what he's feeling. I know when he wants a hug but won't ask.

Our relationship has evolved over the years as we've matured as individuals and as a couple. I like to say that Jack didn't grow up until his fifties. Until then, he always was happy-go-lucky, enjoying sports, staying out with the guys having drinks. But watching him deepen his relationship with God in the years after the Pink House has been nothing short of amazing.

Our lives have always centered on our faith, but that faith has kept growing unbelievably stronger year after year. Now, our faith has become so strong that no matter what happens to us we know we always will stay together and work it out. We support each other totally.

If you live like that, if you support each other and your faith is strong, you can make it through life gracefully no matter what is handed to you.

I encourage you to read this book again and again. Reflect and discover the Secrets and Lessons revealed in your own life. Take time to get to know Jack as I do. Then you will know what to say when asked, "Do you know Jack?"

Bless you!
—Paula Manilla

CHAPTER 1
Saltwater

"Otherwise, you might say in your heart,
It is my own power and the strength of my own hand
that has got me this wealth."
(Deuteronomy 8:17)

Ship on the Sea of Life

After years working as a staffer for Fortune 500 and midsized corporations, I began another career as a business partner and entrepreneur. We grew this business rapidly, and within a few years our profits were approaching $20 million.

Then one day our salespeople started coming to me and questioning their commission earnings. I asked my partner about it, and he fluffed it off, saying it was an accounting error; he claimed that the salespeople were not estimating and tracking correctly and that the orders were incurring heavy labor overtime hour overruns that were needed to meet client delivery schedules.

This went on for several months, and I started tracking and looking deeper into the order costs. I noticed excessive labor costs were in fact being charged to the sales orders. I asked my partner to explain the bookkeeping charges, and I did not get a straight answer. I listened quietly as he tried to bamboozle me with numbers. I began thinking about how he would invite me and my wife, Paula, to his home for parties and out to dinner with his wife at fine restaurants, always picking up the tab. I observed he was living an increasingly higher standard of living. And his wife was wearing new diamonds and pearl jewelry.

A few weeks later during our morning daily coffee time in his office, it was our custom to share current business issues and discuss response strategies. With the door closed he began praising and congratulating me on my performance in growing the business so rapidly. He patted me on the back and handed me a large check, saying it was a bonus reward for my hard work. He then said quietly, "I'm cutting you in for a bigger piece of the action." He went on to say he was issuing me additional stock in the business. I was ecstatic. I couldn't wait to call Paula with the news.

When I finished my coffee, I got up and opened the office door to leave, ... and then he said, "Oh, Jack, there is just one thing," motioning me to close the door and return.

Lowering his voice to almost a whisper... "You'll have to keep your mouth shut."

I said, "What?"

He repeated, ... "You'll have to keep your mouth shut about the labor charges."

He finally admitted it.

I looked at him but for a few seconds, and I resigned on the spot.

He took the check from my hand and tore it up in front of me.

In the movies, these kinds of decisions come with loud musical crescendos. Not so in real life. Within a few months Paula and I lost all the riches that we had accumulated in life. I was left with just my name, ethics, and integrity.

The next five years were some of the hardest financial times Paula and I endured during our marriage. But this period helped define us. We had moved from the mountain of worldly success to the pit of despair. Highly leveraged, Paula and I were forced to sell our three homes and lost all our equity.

Our stone-faced ranch was in an exclusive gated country-club community a few miles from the beaches of the Gulf of Mexico. Lushly landscaped it had a screened, solar-heated swimming pool and an outdoor living area that looked over a tee box, fairway, and green of one of the two private golf courses. We had long enjoyed watching players tee off, hit their fairway shots, head to the green and putt, while we sipped evening cocktails by the pool.

We had completely remodeled the home's interior, upgrading the kitchen and bathrooms and fully screened the outdoor living area after moving to Florida from Milford, Connecticut, in 1991.

In Milford, we had owned a 4,500 square-foot home near the Duck Pond. We also owned a townhome in a private country-club community on picturesque Lake Mohawk in Northeast New Jersey, located in the Sparta Mountains, which border the Pennsylvania Poconos and the Delaware Water Gap National Recreation Area. We kept two boats at the lake —one was a pontoon, and I used a borrowed a name when christening it, *LeBarge Parté*. Summer weekends were filled with many good times on the water, partying with friends.

We also owned a third place in partnership with our daughter, Jackie, and son-in-law, Skip; it was a condominium in Tampa, Florida, where our youngest son lived while going to college. These luxurious residences were now all gone—along with our lavish lifestyle—except for the remaining Florida home we were living in.

I had delayed selling our custom-made Steinway piano for as long as I could. It was our last extravagance, but we had to sell it to pay the real estate agent's commission and the closing costs when we sold this last house.

The baby grand had been hand-built for us. At Steinway Hall in New York City, Paula selected one-of-a-kind French walnut wood for the cabinet. It took eight months to make it. Each week Steinway sent us photographs of the work in progress and invited us to visit the factory to observe their artisans handcrafting our piano. The day it was delivered, I'd exclaimed to Paula that this was my … "Super Bowl Ring"—my trophy of life success.

Advertising the piano for sale I received only one offer. It was a lowball one, and I had a hard time bringing myself to accept it. I searched for other means to come up with the closing monies, but failed. A few days before the closing, with no other place to turn, I accepted the offer of $10,000—a fraction of the original cost.

I was devastated when the buyer picked it up. I watched his crew disassemble it in front me. They removed the legs, secured the soundboard and strings, wrapped it in heavy padding, loaded it onto a piano cart, and wheeled it out of the house to the moving truck. My trophy of worldly success was taken away—gone forever—in minutes right before my eyes…Poof!

We donated many possessions to charity and sold some of our household items and furnishings. We put a few choice pieces of furniture in storage along with Paula's good dinner china, which we had used for entertaining. Some sets had been in Paula's family for generations. Still, the day we closed on the sale of the house, we were very deeply in debt.

We packed our suitcases and spent the last night at the house. Early the next morning, we rose at 5:00 a.m. to attend morning Mass as was now our habit.

My entire life, I had lived by the saying… "God never gives you more than you can handle." *Now, man up! Fix it! Forward! And Act!* But that morning I couldn't fix anything. I was totally defeated.

The Secret: "Seek first the kingdom [of God] and his righteousness, and all these things will be given you besides." (Matthew 6:25–34)

The Lesson: "We squander health in search of wealth. We scheme and toil and save, then squander wealth in search of health and all we get is a grave. We live and boast of what we own, we die and only get a stone." (Billy Graham)

Most of us have our priorities backward. We seek material things most of our lives, storing up for retirement and look forward to living what is called the good life. At some point, we must come to realize that material things have not fully satisfied our deepest inner longings.

I was about to learn the answer to this longing. The answer would come over the next eighteen months when I strove to find the deeper meanings in life and my purpose for earthly.

The answer was simple. It is found while one strives for the eternal, for the spiritual, the Kingdom. It is only then that we begin to be truly satisfied and experience true peace, love, and joy. The more we move in this direction, the more happiness we will receive.

The Secret: Store treasures in heaven. "Do not store up for yourselves treasures on earth, where moth and decay destroy, and thieves break in and steal. But store up treasures in heaven, where neither moth nor decay destroys, nor thieves break in and steal. For where your treasure is, there also will your heart be" (Matthew 6:19–21).

The Lesson: The best investments we can make are in the First National Bank of Heaven. Upon life's exodus, the return on investment (ROI), will last for all eternity.

December 15, 1994

I awoke Thursday morning at 5:30am, the day after we sold our home. Dawn had not yet broken the dark of night. During the four months since I had resigned Paula and I had developed the habit of going to the 6:30 a.m. daily morning Mass. I had interviewed for jobs with several large corporations, but no offers came. I was distraught. I had always quickly righted our ship when strife occurred. This time we were shipwrecked, our barque destroyed by a tsunami from the storm on the saltwater sea of life four months ago.

We washed up on the shore and were lost like dust in the sand at a small Florida town known as *Safety Harbor* ... True Name... located in the Northwest corner of Tampa Bay.

At 6:00 am Paula and I entered the dimly lighted Espiritu Santo Catholic Church (Church of the Holy Spirit) Safety Harbor, Florida, and stepped into an empty pew. We knelt in silent prayer. A dozen people were scattered about the church. Our pew was two-thirds back from the altar to the right of the center aisle, and I was on the outside next to the aisle; Paula to my right. We continued kneeling and praying silently with bowed heads as we waited for the morning Mass to begin.

This morning I was about to have the most amazing, unforgettable experience of a lifetime. Events of that morning would confirm forever my belief of all things visible and invisible—

"I believe in one God, the Father Almighty,
maker of heaven and earth,
of all things, visible and invisible."
(Nicene Creed, Profession of the Christian - Faith Part 1)
(Catechism of the Catholic Church, Section 2)

This morning I would be rescued.

> **The Secret:** "For a whole year they met with the church (in Antioch) and taught a large number of people, and it was in Antioch that the disciples were first called Christians." (Acts 11:26)

> **The Lesson:** Who were the first Christians? The disciples were first called Christians at Antioch because they *walked and talked like Jesus.*

While praying that morning I was reflecting on what had become of our lives as the result of that one critical decision a few months past. I kept saying to myself, *"I did the right thing."* I had confronted my business partner on his wrongdoings and would not, could not, compromise my values, ethics, honesty, and integrity. I knew I was morally right and just, in making the decision to resign. *It was the right thing to do!* But why must I now have lost everything but the love of Paula, family, and close friends who stood by and supported us.

I held these thoughts in my heart, and shared them silently with the Lord. I was never a big complainer, and I viewed a glass of water as always, half full, not half empty. But my glass was empty.

I was fifty-three years old, our wealth gone, my business career crashed. I wondered, Is my work career over? Shipwrecked, blown onto the rocks by the raging storm of the saltwater sea of life and lost. All was lost... or so I thought. I could not man up. I could not fix it!

> **The Secret:** "Better to be poor and walk in integrity than rich and crooked in one's ways." (Proverbs 19:1)

> **The Lesson:** "Life is not about learning how to survive in the storm, but learning how to dance in the rain." (Author unknown).

A.J. Russell in his book *God Calling* reflects on the story of Jesus asleep in the boat when a storm arises, "In the spiritual (as in the material) world, there is no empty space, and as self and fears and worries depart out of your lives, it follows that the things of the Spirit, love, joy and happiness that you crave, will rush in to take their places.

Be not afraid. Fear not. It is to the drowning man the *Rescuer* comes. To the brave *swimmer* who can fare well alone He comes not. And no rush of Joy can be like that of a man toward his *Rescuer*.

It is part of God's method to wait until the storm is at its full violence (before rescue). Jesus could have bid the first angry wave be calm, the first gust of wind be still, but what a lesson unlearned. The sense of (God's) nearness of refuge and safety would have been lost.

Remember this: (the) disciples thought that in sleep (Jesus) had forgotten them. Remember how mistaken they were. Gain strength and confidence and joyful dependence and anticipation from that. Never fear. Joy is yours, and the radiant joy of the rescued shall be yours."

CHAPTER 2
Holy Water

"I am the Lord, your God, teaching you how to prevail,
leading you on the way you should go."
(Isaiah 48:17)

Holy Water

I blessed myself with holy water on entering church that morning of December 15, 1994, just as I had for years before. As I did I thought about a Protestant friend I once nvited to come with me to Sunday Mass. He had asked about the holy water fonts placed near the church entrance.

Why did we dip our fingers in the fonts and make the sign of the cross when we entered and left the church? I said it was a historical tradition. We place fonts of holy water near the entrances of our churches, like the Old Testament Jewish practices of purification when entering and leaving the Temple. Three reasons we have fonts filled with holy water for blessings are:

1. As a sign of repentance of sin
2. For protection from evil
3. As a reminder of our baptism

Just as water and blood flowed from the sacred heart of our Lord as He hung upon the cross, signifying the great sacraments of baptism and the Holy Eucharist of the Last Supper, the taking of holy water and making the sign of the cross before Mass is to remind us of our baptism in preparation for the reception of the Holy Eucharist.

While kneeling in the pew waiting for mass to begin, I closed my eyes and prayed fervently for deliverance.

Lord hear me, help me.
I never killed anyone and I am no Billy Graham or Mother Teresa either.
I totally surrender my will to you this day.

I went on to tell God,

I give up. I can't do it myself. I am sincerely sorry. I apologize
for living my life in the driver's seat and keeping you, the
Lord God, in the back seat. I beg for mercy. Forgive me.

Most of my life I tenaciously worked for money,
power, and prestige. I identified who I was by these
and now was beginning to realize that they meant
and did nothing but fuel my pride, my ego.
I asked Jesus to show me the way out of this dilemma.

"Help me! I am drowning!"

The Secret: "My soul is downcast within me ...
Deep calls to deep in the roar of your torrents,
and all your waves and breakers sweep over me."
(Psalm 42:6–7)

I appealed to all the saints to please intercede on my behalf,
reciting a litany of centuries-old names. When I could remember
no more, I asked the angels for their help, pleading to my guardian
angel and to the archangels: Michael, Gabriel, and Raphael. As soon
as I said the archangel's names thoughts came instantaneously to
me, *"Michael and Gabriel, you are popular choices for preachers, but I
don't think I've ever heard anyone talk about you, Raphael, you must be
very lonely. No one much thinks of you, talks about you or asks you for
help."*

"Raphael, I need your help. I need it now!"
I never prayed so hard in my life.

In earlier times, it was common belief that inexplicable events
were due to the actions of spiritual beings. This has given way
to current scientific world views and a different sense of cause
and effect. Yet spiritual believers still experience God's protection,
communication, and guidance in ways that defy description. We
cannot dismiss angels too lightly.

"Suppose they do not believe me or listen to me?
For they may say, "The LORD did not appear to you."
(Exodus 4:1)

The Secret: "God heard and listened to my voice."
Blessed be God, who did not reject my prayer and
refuse his mercy." (Psalm 66:19–20)

Still kneeling, I felt a strong urge to open my eyes and look to
the front of the church. A cloud-like mist filled and enveloped the
altar sanctuary. The rising sun was just starting to cast its glow,
and my eyes were drawn upward to the large round stained glass
window with a dove in the center. Suddenly, a brilliant sunbeam
shone through the glass, and amazing colors illuminated the
sanctuary. My eyes followed the sunbeam like a spotlight down
through the heavy mist to the altar table. It illuminated and cleared
an elliptical opening in the mist around the table.

There in the illuminated clearing stood a man to the left of the
altar, mid-twenties in age, with short, jet-black, curly hair. I thought
he was an altar server preparing to light the candles for morning
Mass… But *he was strangely dressed.* He was not in a black, ankle-
length cassock with a white cotta top, but was dressed *in an all-white
toga* that reached just below the knees. He just stood there staring
at the altar table. Puzzled, I thought, *who is he? What is he doing?
What am I seeing?* I blinked and rubbed my eyes several times. He
was still there, looking at the altar. This is not a man. *I saw an angel.*

The Secret: "His appearance was like lightning
and his clothing was white as snow." (Matthew
28:3)

No sooner had I completed the thought, I was seeing an
angel, than the being turned and looked straight at me, coal-black
eyes penetrated deeply into mine. It was surreal, like nothing I'd

ever experienced. Time stood still, no words spoken, our minds merged, locked together for several minutes, like a magnet. He was telling me something but not with spoken words. It was strangely telepathic (like a "mind meld" by the character Spock in the TV series *Star Trek*). I heard in my mind,

> "And your ears shall hear a word behind
> you, an angelic announcement."
> (Isaiah 30:21)

He next turned slowly to his left and again looked directly at the altar table, it seemed for several minutes. I watched in silent wonder…Then

> **The Secret:** "I heard behind me a voice as loud as
> a trumpet." (Revelation 1:10)

> "I'll be with you."
> (Exodus 3:12)

> "See, I am sending an angel before you, to guard you on the way
> and bring you to the place I have prepared."
> (Exodus 23:20"

> **The Lesson**: "I, Jesus, sent my angel to give you
> this testimony for the churches. I am the root and
> offspring of David, the bright morning star. The
> Spirit and the bride say, 'Come.'" Let the hearer say,
> 'Come.' Let the one who thirsts come forward, and
> the one who wants it, receive the gift of life-giving
> water. (Revelation 22:16–17)

> **The Secret:** Almost instantly I felt a sharp, pointed
> tap on my left shoulder.

I quickly turned my head left to the aisle, thinking someone tapped ma as they wanted to enter the pew. No one was there.

I looked back to the door of the church entrance, no one.

I looked up the aisle to the altar. No one.

I looked all about. The angel and mist had gone, vanished from sight.

I looked to the pews directly behind me in front of me and all around. No one.

I thought, *someone who tapped me took a different pew,* but no one new had come into the church.

I looked to my right. Paula was still kneeling in prayer. I looked again up and down the aisle and to the altar, full sun was now illuminating the church. Nothing.

I quietly asked Paula, *"Did you see that?"*

She replied, "See what?"

"The mist around the altar!"

"No."

"Did you see the man in the toga?"

"No."

"Did you hear that?"

"Hear what?"

"The voice!"

She looked deeply into my eyes and answered, "No."

I asked her, *"Did you tap my shoulder?"*

"No," she said.

I closed my eyes and replayed everything in my mind that had just occurred. It was, is, and will forever be a permanent hologram in the museum of my mind.

> "On the day I cried out,
> you answered;
> you strengthened my spirit."
> (Psalms 138:3)

God sent an angel, he appeared, spoke and touched me. The message:

"I'll Be with You!"

Then the messenger disappeared.

"I have seen the messenger of the LORD!"

Am I hallucinating? Is something wrong with me?

"The Lord answered him."
(Judges 6:22)

"You are safe. Do not fear."

"I trust in you, LORD;
I say, 'You are my God.'
My destiny is in your hands"
(Psalms 31:15-16)

The next moment the entrance bell rang announcing Mass was beginning. The priest processed with two altar-boys to the sanctuary and prayer services began. I glanced at my watch... 6:30 a.m. Thirty minutes had passed in a blink of an eye.

> **The Lesson:** "I am beside you. Can you feel My Presence? Contact with Me is not gained by the senses. Spirit-consciousness replaces sight. When man sees Me with his human sight, it does not mean of necessity that his spiritual perception is greater. Nay, rather that for that soul I have to span the physical and the spiritual with a spiritual vision clear to human eyes." (A.J. Russell, *God Calling*)

El Roi
"To the Lord who spoke to her she gave the name, saying,
'You are God who sees me'; she meant, "have I really seen
(God's angel) and remained alive after he saw me?"
(Genesis 16:13)

After Mass on the way to our car, I told Paula of my experience.
I again asked if she had seen or heard anything. She squeezed my
hand and said she had not.

"Now go! I am sending you ... I am who I am."
(Exodus 3:10,12,14)

Five minutes later we stopped at our favorite nearby place for
breakfast. The restaurant's name posted on a large outdoor sign:

My Way.

The words loomed large in my mind.

The Secret: Jesus finds and rescues us. "Behold,
I am with you always, until the end of the age."
(Matthew 28:10)

"I, Jesus, sent my angel to give you this testimony for the
churches. I am the root and offspring of David, the bright morning
star." The Spirit and the bride say, "Come." Let the hearer say,
"Come." Let the one who thirsts come forward, and the one who
wants it receive the gift of life-giving water." (Revelation 22:16–17)

My Way... Huh! A short time ago, I had surrendered my will,
experienced a theophany, and now this restaurant sign was glaring
at me. Paula and I talked during our meal, and I asked her what she
thought about my description of the experience I'd had before Mass.
She calmly looked into my eyes and replied, "I don't really know. I am

probably as dismayed as you at the events taking place in our lives. No matter what happens I am with you, and I love you, forever and ever." Paula is amazingly strong and loving. She is a very special woman.

After eating we got on the road, and an hour later as I turned off the main highway, I glanced at the signpost. I had driven here before but never thought much about the name of the road, but everything about this day was different. Huh! Lake Patience Road.

I drove on and came to a four-way stop where we were to turn. I saw another sign posted in a field with a directional arrow. Huh! Lake Destiny!

I turned onto a gravel road that led us deep into the middle of an orange grove and pulled up on the grass in front of a 1930s' Florida cracker bungalow painted pink—the Pink House!

I sat in the car a while, looking at the orange trees and that bungalow thinking about everything that had happened in the past six months. Months later as I reflected on this moment, l thought this is what Jesus's disciples must have been thinking and how they felt during their walk back to Emmaus from Jerusalem on that first Easter evening. I thought of the issues at my former workplace, the sale of our homes, the *apparition,* the three posted signs: My Way, Lake Patience Road, and Lake Destiny.

My life, who and what I identified as self, was no more. I literally thought I was like the dew wafting into a misty vapor. I wondered what the future would bring.

I would reflect on these things not only for a few months but for the rest of my life, the apparition, My Way, Patience, and Destiny.

"For by grace you have been saved through faith, and this is not from you; it is the gift of God; it is not from works, so no one may boast. For we are his handiwork, created in Christ Jesus for the good works that God has prepared in advance, that we should live in them."
(Ephesians 2:8–10)

The Pink House became my monastery, a spiritual gymnasium, and classroom. The orange grove was my outdoor field track. Twice a day, in the early mornings and late evenings, I would pray, read scripture, and walk through the orange grove, listening to the birds, watching the squirrels and the oranges patiently grow. Many people think an orange is an orange; but there are several types of oranges, some best for juice, others best for eating. Oranges have different flavors, depending on which state or country they are grown. This Florida grove's trees were juicers that bore fruit twice each year and were harvested in the fall and spring. A thought came to me one morning that we humans are like all different orange types, and I wondered in what seasons do we each bear fruit throughout our lives. Some bear none. Some are over abundant. *What am I?*

During the first few weeks as I walked through the orange grove, I raised my fist, looking at the sky and in anger and anxiety, shouting aloud over and over, "I did the right thing! Why am I being punished? Why are we in this orange grove? Why? Why? Why?" I raged.

Then one morning as I was finishing my orange grove walk, frustrated, I shouted aloud to the heavens, "How long must I wait in this Pink House? When will I get a job? What am I to do? How will I pay back all the money I owe?" On and on I went ranting. I then said, "I am thirsty for answers. God Help me!" I then went inside The Pink House and read the day's Bible verses and devotional reflection from *Our Daily Bread*.

> **The Secret**: I read, "How long must I wait (for you)? ... I am thirsty." (John 19:28)

The words cut me like a sword run through. At that moment, God spoke directly to my heart. He turned my question around and directed it right back at me,

The Lesson: I kept reading, "Then the Lord spoke to Job out of the storm. He said, Who is this who darkens counsel with words of ignorance? Gird up your loins now, like a man; I will question you, and you tell me the answers!" (Job 38:1–39:30)

A chill went up my spine! I answered aloud, "Yes, Lord, I am yours. show me what to do. "

Thus, began an intense discipline. In the following months, I would read scripture and walk daily through the orange grove, predawn and dusk, meditating on the Bible passages, talking openly to God about everything and reflecting on the Word. The questions God posed of Job struck me personally, and I thought how he learned to see the wisdom of God as shown in the creation around him.

The too-busy lives we allow ourselves to live permit little time for simple pleasures like those daily orange grove walks. Be jealous of your time. Enjoy life's simple pleasures. Take nature walks.

The Orange Grove

To best describe the following months, I would have to take you with me to experience a cool predawn walk through a Florida orange grove. Feel the refreshing warmth of the morning sun on your face. See the solar heat transform dew into misty vapors wafting in the air, where instantly in my mind I would relive my angel in the mist. I was like the dew and changing to vapor. My old life wafted with the mist into the air. Now listen to our steps scatter the squirrels and birds from their nests as we breathe in the heady fragrance of fresh orange blossoms. To this day now, every time I peel open an orange and breathe in the citrus smell these memories envelope me. Peel one yourself and there—that smell, that taste—that's the taste of my transformation in the orange grove and my Pink House experience. In an orange grove, you can get completely lost; and find exactly what you've been looking for all your life. There, Jesus will find and rescue you.

> "Life's about morning walks and lengthy talks. Smelling flowers, enjoying showers. For writing books, exploring nooks. I'll squander not my health or wealth. For when I die, I'll call your bluff. I'll leave my thoughts, instead, instead of stuff."
> (Patricia Lorenz, author, *Daily Guideposts*)

It would take months to change me. In time I lost my anger, became at peace, felt rested, even experienced moments of joy. Periodically Paula would ask me, "Well, which should we do, pay this bill or buy groceries?" Our dwindling small savings almost gone. Negative thoughts would leak into my consciousness and rush over me like huge ocean waves. For months I was in a battle of positive over negative, good over evil. At times at complete peace in the orange grove. At other times, it was like the movie *Groundhog Day*. I was repeating the same events over and over in my mind. I was like those men on the road to Emmaus.

I was clinging for survival. It felt like I was on a rocky beach with large ocean waves pounding and washing over me and onto the sand, the water slowly ebbing and flowing back to sea as the energy of the waves dissipated. Then one day it changed. A large wave came in, knocked me loose of my hold and tumbled my body over and over in the surf of despair.

Many years later during the Lenten season I was reflecting on the experience of the *Miracle in the Mist*, this as I have done every day since that eventful December morning. I was contemplating the first Easter Day two thousand years ago when everyone was looking for Jesus.

The women rose before dawn and went to the tomb to anoint the body, found it empty, and cried out, "He is gone!" (Mark 16:1–8) They ran to the tell the disciples, who were hiding in the locked upper room, no doubt frightened that the Roman guard would soon find and arrest them too (Mark 16:14–18), Peter, John, and Mary Magdalene saying to each other, "Where is He?" (John 20:10) (Please see in the appendix *Pilate's Letter to Tiberius Caesar Concerning Arrest, Trial, and Crucifixion of Jesus.*)

I imagined in my mind's eye the citizens and visitors in the city of Jerusalem during those days, frightened in response to armed Roman soldiers rushing about the entire city, kicking in doors, turning furnishings over, and questioning everyone, "Where is he? Did you take him? Did you see anyone carrying a body?"

The Roman soldiers had been instructed by their superiors to find Jesus's body or else suffer severe consequences. They were desperate, and after many hours of looking everywhere and finding nothing, they reluctantly returned to report their failure. Their superiors told them to wait outside while they discussed their fate. They must have been frightened. Finally, a decision was agreed to and money given to the soldiers to keep them quiet and they were instructed to tell the people that Jesus's disciples stole and hid the body (Matthew 28:11–15).

Later that same day in the afternoon, two men were talking as they were walking on the road to Emmaus. Totally disillusioned and trying to understand what they had witnessed in Jerusalem. They reviewed the recent week's events, the triumphant entry of Jesus into the city and then but a few days later the crucifixion (Luke 24:13–35).

On that first day of Easter the stories all tell … the risen one does the finding. In the shadows of predawn and near-sunset, Jesus finds those deepest in confusion and grief. Many volumes have been written, church decrees issued, and countless sermons preached on the nature and history of the resurrection. But notice, for those who deeply love the Lord, …

Jesus does the finding… He finds the grieving. He finds us, as we've all been "Emmaus walkers" at some point in our lives, when the crushing waves from storms on the sea of life envelope us. But it's in the shadow times like this that the risen Christ finds us and brings us to the eye of the storm, a place of peace and safety.

In my case, that place of safety was the Pink House. Know that you walk in good company. Stop running about searching for Jesus. Take a stand. Wait patiently and in silent listening. The risen one will find you … near the dawn or dusk. He's been doing it that way since the very first Easter day. Jesus will find you! Let Him know you are ready to be found.

> **The Secret:** At this moment, I recalled the angel in the mist and knew with certainty I was rescued. It was then I truly believed the angel message delivered that December morning.

> "I have told you this so that you might have peace in me. In the world, you will have trouble, but take courage, I have conquered the world." (John 16:33)

> "Do not fear: I am with you; do not be anxious: I am your God. I will strengthen you, I will help you." (Isaiah 41:10)

> **The Lesson:** "The Lord promises peace, but not leisure, heart-rest and comfort, but not pleasure." (A. J. Russell, *God Calling*)

I touched base with dozens of business contacts I had made over the years, looking for leads. After a few more months of prospecting, I went on a number of job interviews. I thought, *Well, here we go. I'll soon be back on track.* Within a few weeks after the vetting process by each, I was recommended by the presidents of three different large manufacturers to become their heirs apparent. Meetings were set with the board chairs of each firm. I went for a haircut, changed from shorts, tees, and sandals to my best business suit and flew around the country on separate trips from Florida to Austin, Texas, to Philadelphia, Pennsylvania, and to Atlanta, Georgia. On each trip I was met at the airport by limo drivers, stayed in fine hotels, and dined in exquisite restaurants with my future employers as they grilled me.

Then I would return to the Pink House. Paula anxiously waited to hear all about my trip. Together we waited for a job offer. Living near Lake Patience Road, I kept telling myself, *Patience, patience, patience.* I expected a call each day, but none came. Not even a courtesy call to say, "Thank you for your time, but we selected someone else." Strike one, strike two, strike three. Three strikes all in a row. I struck out.

I kept asking God, "Why?" I had done the right thing ethically, confronted wrongdoing, refused to compromise my ethics, and resigned. Why was I being punished? Depressed again, thinking my business career was over, I said to Paula that I was thinking of applying for a job at Walmart as a greeter and that we should begin looking for a double-wide.

One day, months later, the answer came to me. I finally realized I had not truly changed. I kept trying do it my way and not God's way. I kept trying to go back to Egypt to rejoin my old life. My Way is not self-way. My Way is God's way.

I stopped the intermittent complaining and finally gave up my anger. Once again I humbled myself saying, "God, I'm truly sorry for how I've been complaining these past few months. Please accept my apology. I think I am beginning to understand. 'My Way' is not Jack's way. My Way is your way." When I said this, all stress left from my body like a great weight lifted off my shoulders, and a calm, relaxing, comforting, refreshing peace enveloped me.

I prayed intently for forgiveness for having lived my life by the words of the song "My Way" written by Paul Anka and sung by Frank Sinatra, "I did it my way." Now again in total complete surrender, I let go and truly let God. I promised I would no longer "do it my way, but do it your way." I was and still am in many respects a very stubborn person.

I now felt even more drawn to read the Bible. I continued to read the Bible completely through, cover to cover, three times within six weeks, and I did so each day before and after my orange grove walks.

The first time through, I read it through like a history novel, drawn into the stories, not able to put it down. The words amazingly flowed quickly and easily, resonating deep within me day after day. It was a marvelous time. I was acquiring new knowledge, new understanding, transforming.

I had read short passages in the Bible off and on occasionally over the past twenty years, but the words never had the depth of meaning I was now experiencing. By the third time through, the words leaped from the pages into my mind with new understanding. I felt like I was having conversations with God. I would be thinking something and then read a direct reply. My mind freely floated as thoughts would enter and scripture collaborated. I was given a precious gift—enlightenment. I was growing, maturing in knowledge, understanding, and discernment.

As I read the Bible stories and then went into the orange grove, I reflected on my past experiences and how closely they resembled those of them who lived in ancient times. They had encountered similar circumstances. I identified with how they must have felt and what their thoughts might have been. History was repeating itself with me. But now, as a result, was I really learning and changing? I discovered that over and over when the ancient people would turn away from their pleasures and materialistic ways to living God's way, they would find rest, peace, love, and happiness.

It seemed to me that Bible history was repeating itself in my life. I thought of Moses and the Israelites and wondered what they must have been thinking and what they were saying to each other when they were wandering lost in the desert. Frustrated and angry, full of anxiety, they longed for their former lives, to the point of rebelling, even if it meant returning to a life of Egyptian slavery, or in my case to a world of corporate slavery in the pursuit of endlessly increasing the top and bottom lines.

As I settled into a new daily routine, pondering the scriptures on my walks through the orange grove, I reflected on the details, over and over, about the angel in the mist and the restaurant sign, My Way, and the street signs: Lake Patience and Lake Destiny.

Here I was living in a bungalow called the Pink House and walking through the orange grove. Were these all but ordinary coincidences? I came to think of these as "co-incidents," envisioning both heaven and earthly forces simultaneously fusing like lightning bolts to create a unique, instantaneous occurrence.

Not knowing where Paula and I would go or what do to earn a living, I came to truly trust God completely for my future, no matter what. I mean I truly, completely, with absolutely no reservations, doubts, or second thoughts understood my future was now and would always be totally in His hands.

> **The Secret:** "Aspire to live a tranquil life, to mind your own affairs, and to work with your hands, as we instructed you, that you may conduct yourselves properly toward outsiders and not depend on anyone." (1 Thessalonians 4:11–12)

> **The Lesson:** Live in the present. Live simply.

> "Yesterday is history. Tomorrow is a mystery, and today is a gift; that's why they call it the present."
> (Eleanor Roosevelt)

My new daily habit was formed. I continue to this day to rise from sleep before dawn to pray, read scripture, meditate, contemplate, journal, and reflect on the amazing angel in the mist event and repeat, "But Mary said to the angel, 'How can this be?'" (Luke 1:34)

How can this be? I pondered the meaning of the angel's movements, his looking at the church altar, looking into my eyes, looking back once more to the altar. God had spoken to me through the voice of the archangel, "I'll be with you." He had confirmed it with a sharp touch on my shoulder. *Was this real? Did it really happen?* It did. It happened. I experienced three distinct physical confirmations of it: sight, hearing, and touch.

I questioned myself. Was I the same person I had been? I read story after story of the mystics, saints, and fathers of the church. I was not holy like them. I was not being called to be like them? Or was I? For what purpose?

Then one morning, just before sunrise while I was contemplating all these things, the meaning of the angel's movements was revealed to me.

"And the angel said to her (him) in reply,
"'The Holy Spirit will come upon you,'"
(Luke 1:35)

A moment before I had returned in my mind to Espiritu Santo Church, Safety Harbor, Florida, December 15, 1994. I recalled how I had emptied myself in total surrender to the will of God.

> **The Secret:** "I say to you, it is easier for a camel to pass through the eye of a needle than for one who is rich to enter the kingdom of God." (Matthew 19:24)

Message Clarity

For years I felt curiously uncomfortable and struggled for conscience clarity of thought regarding the Angel's message, delivered when he stared deeply into my eyes on December 15, 1994. Recall always seemed diffuse.

Then in mid-July of 2016, during my daily morning prayer time, as is my habit I was reflecting on the Miracle *in the Mist* experiences when I had a blessing of remarkable understanding and wrote it down.

In my mind's eye, I was back in the orange grove by the Pink House, when a door suddenly appeared in front of me. As I stood in front of it, I recalled the desperate circumstances I was in on that December morning. I was lost, my future unknown, progress blocked as by a locked, closed door. What was to come of my life from this time on? I had cried out to the Lord, angels, archangels, and saints for help, and at that very moment ... the door automatically unlocked and swung open.

I walked through the door opening, and there I saw an amazingly, large spiral ramp reaching from the earth to the heavens. I stepped onto the base of the ramp, and I was enveloped by complete peace unknown before.

I took a few steps forward but was unable to advance further. I then recalled, all the events of the 18 months living in The Pink House. I recalled as I walked through the orange grove an enormous spiritual thirst had developed within me. Quenched only by reading the Bible. As I thought of scripture words I slowly began to walk up the spiraling ramp.

Many people experience what is called déjà vu and express that their lives seem to be always going in circles. I discovered that both are true. We are not moving along a flat plain of life. Rather we are on a circular, spiraling spiritual ramp.

I saw thousands, upon thousands, of people on the wide spiral, some going up at various speed – walking, jogging, running, some coming down, slipping and sliding tumbling back, some falling off the edge to the bottom and beginning again, some just stopped. Others being led forcibly by angels to the door, tossed out, and the door closed.

Amazing Gifts

My daily orange grove walks had revealed amazing gifts, waiting to surprise as each upper level of the spiral was reached. They are there just around the next bend.

One gift is scripture enlightenment. I acquired it in four stages, and as I unwrapped the gift I advanced further up the spiral ramp.

Stage One—Untying the ribbon
Drawn by great spiritual thirst, I acquired *knowledge* as I read the Bible completely through three times, cover to cover, within six weeks.

Stage Two—Removing the wrapping
I developed *understanding*, an awareness to insightful meanings of the Word of God, revealed by studying small phrases and reflecting on one sentence at a time. New and deeper meanings were derived as the same words were read over and over like the peelings of an onion unfolding in thin layers, little by little.

Stage Three—Opening the box
I acquired a skill in *discerning* scripture as applied to matters of my everyday earthly life.

Stage Four—Embracing the gift
I began a *conversation* with God. The Word spoke to me personally. In the past when I heard others talk of their having a personal relationship with the Lord, I thought it but theological intellectualism. Bible readings, though interesting, always seemed to be as distant as the ancient time they were recorded. I questioned and rationalized how these words could possibly relate directly to me in the here and now? But now I too was given this great gift.

"Oh, the depth of the riches and wisdom and knowledge of God!"
(Romans 11:33)

This relationship is available to all. One only needs place themselves into what I call *Listening Prayer*. (I will explain this later in chapter 5.) It is acquired and developed by exercising the spiritual mind daily.

As I continued up the ramp, other gifts, like sparks of God's divine power and bursts of supernatural energy, kept me going onward and upward. Some call this grace, and it is available 24/7/365. All one need do is turn self-off, plug into the divine power source as we do our smartphones, and recharge.

Plugging in is done by simply abiding with God in personal prayer, meditation on scripture, and contemplation. Receiving Holy Communion provides a supercharge.

I observed the thousands of people along the spiral, they all were walking at different speeds. Some were jogging, some were running past, others seemed in slow motion, while some stood still.

As long as we keep God's commandments, remain meek and humble, study to increase our spiritual knowledge, continuous transformation will occur, and each will advance in maturity at our own speeds and paces to the next level of the spiraling ramp.

But beware. We stop to ascend when worldly pride, judgment and sin re-enter our lives. Depending on the degree of worldliness that we allow, we will slip and slide, may tumble and roll back down the ramp, and even fall off the ramp. I saw some being turned back into the temporal world. Angels were picking up those that had fallen off the ramp and tossing them back out the door. The door was then closed behind them and locked.

Remember: doors open both ways. Beware!

The Lesson: "Seek the LORD, all you humble of the land, who have observed his law; Seek justice, seek humility; Perhaps you will be sheltered." (Zephaniah 2:3)

All are invited to come to the banquet table of the Lord. There is a place at table waiting for everyone. It is reserved in churches all around the world here and now. The main Lord's Table is a Long Table, and it is at the top of the spiral.

I was invited to ascend to the top of the spiritual ramp, walk through the gates into the Holy City, and enter the house of the Lord. There, I was drawn to an immense inner room engulfed in that same cloud-like mist I had seen years before, but in lieu of a single bright sunbeam, a brilliant white, centering light and amazing colors illuminated the mist. Overhead, countless thousands of tiny floating, golden, flame-like sparks were flying into the room.

Then I saw it—*The Long Table*, an endless banquet table sweeping in very elongated curves, on out into infinity in both directions. Angels were escorting thousands of people one-by-one to reserved seats at the table. Other angels were unfolding and placing white tablecloths.

This was followed by the placement of hundreds of golden candelabras and as the tiny floating, golden, flame-like sparks came to rest on candelabras they burst into dancing candle flames. Then an opening appeared in the mist, revealing choir groups of singing angels, arrayed in sections along the Long Table.

"And suddenly there was a multitude of the heavenly host
with the angel, praising God and saying: Glory to God in the
highest and on earth peace to those on whom His favor rests."
(Luke 2:13–14)

"They name him Wonder-Counselor, God-Hero,
Father-Forever, Prince of Peace."
(Isaiah 9:5)

Just as suddenly, there appeared before me my angel of the *Miracle in the Mist*, gesturing to take an open seat at the long table.

I sat down and joined the thousands of joyful saints singing in communion with the angels and abiding in unexplainable joy and love, in ecstasy, with the Father, Son, and Holy Spirit.

Unforgettable.

"You have let me experience the joys of life and the exquisite pleasures of your own eternal prescience."
(Psalm 16:11, TLB)

Just as suddenly I was back in the orange grove and quickly back in our home in Jacksonville—amazing!

Ever since that revelation, the daily walk on the circular ascent has been an exciting spiritual adventure, lasting me a lifetime into God's supernatural world of peace, love, and joy.

Some people I have shared this experience with have said it may have been a dream you created on your own. Well, if it was or was not, I know in my heart it is what I what I saw and heard and many believe life in heaven will be like. And the lives being lived on earth today are graphically depicted by those on the Spiritual Spiral Ramp.

> **The Secret:** "I have much more to tell you, but you cannot bear it now." (John 16:12)

> **The Lesson:** When we surrender *self,* we think, *Well, I'm in 100 percent. I've turned everything over to the Lord.* But my personal experience is otherwise. It is not easy, we must *fully* surrender every day.

There are multiple layers of self-buried deep within us. Only over time as we search ourselves do we discover them. When we find them, we must surrender each one. As we do God uses them to shape the new us in preparation for eternity with Him.

When Christ died on the cross, the total human self-surrendered as the body was crucified. Three days later, He conquered death and rose. As we conquer our human self we gain supernatural power and are released from the burdens of the world. It is then we find peace.

It is not the difficulties of earthly life we must conquer, but the self within us.

As we learn God's teachings, obey His commands, abiding and listening to His guidance on our "Emmaus walk," we will see marvelous revelations.

Paula and I now live simply, which is dramatically different from our former life. We are blessed to drive new cars again. We can easily succumb to a life of complexity and the never-ending media appeal, tempting our material desires to accumulate stuff. We now seek to satisfy the spiritual desire, a thirst, a longing that is difficult to define and express with worldly stuff.

The stress and tension of life can become so intense at times it can prevent us from really enjoying life. I came to realize a happy life is really about simplicity.

Our son Paul has been doing so for years, and observing him has greatly influenced our lifestyle. This was not an easy thing to do, to yield my free will. I was always very stubborn, and when I focused on a goal, I was unrelenting in achieving it.

As they say It was my way or the highway. I overcame this test by becoming aware of my hubris. Then regularly recalling to mind the large restaurant sign...*MY WAY*... is *God's Way*.

Reading the scriptures, reflecting on them, meditating, contemplating and considering my past and present life, I came to realize I was just like the Israelites of thousands of years ago.

I had been wandering in the desert, searching for my promised land for forty years. I had been riding a merry-go-round of life, reaching for the golden ring that promised a free ride.

I was struck by the thought that this was exactly what the Israelites must have been thinking, and this is how they must have felt, having lost everything, journeyed off into the desert on a forty-year trip that should have taken only eleven days. They mourned for years to return to Egypt, while longing at the same time for the Promised Land.

While in the orange grove, I shouted, "Lord, how much longer must I wait for my Promised Land? I am thirsty!"

I no sooner asked this when instantly the following response was spoken to me in the silence of my mind. I was startled and shaken by the profoundness.

How long must I wait for you? I am thirsty.

> **The Secret:** "Then Jesus said to his disciples, 'Whoever wishes to come after me must deny himself, take up his cross, and follow me. For whoever wishes to save his life will lose it, but whoever loses his life for my sake will find it. What profit would there be for one to gain the whole world and forfeit his life?" (Matthew 16:24–26)

> **The Lesson:** Make a true commitment to serve God and serve Him first, no matter what. Christianity is not about me. It is about surrender of the self-will and serving God. Serving others is service to God.

> When you are called, do not selfishly question before you commit, asking what is in it for me, what will I get in return, will my life get easier, will I get more? Will this guarantee me a place in heaven?

> Pick up and carry your cross, go where you don't want to go, and do what you would rather not do. It's called obedience.

"I am troubled now. Yet what should I say? 'Father, save me from this hour'? But it was for this purpose that I came to this hour." (John 12:27)

The Secret: "And this is my prayer: that your love may increase ever more and more in knowledge and every kind of perception, to discern what is of value, so that you may be pure and blameless for the day of Christ, filled with the fruit of righteousness that comes through Jesus Christ for the glory and praise of God." (Philippians 1:9–11)

The Lesson: Train yourself for spiritual fitness in the gymnasium of the mind.

Like physical training or therapy, spiritual training must be personalized for different bodies. Spiritual training is also best when personalized for different spirits. It is difficult for one who willingly enjoys a life of solitude and silent prayer but lives an ever-increasing busy work and family life to set aside daily time to exercise the spirit. If this is you, seek and consult a spiritual advisor, mentor, director, or personal trainer to help you develop a personalized plan for spiritual development. The Lord will join you at the gym for your daily workouts when you do.

The Lord intervened in my complex life, removing me from it completely for eighteen months of transformation. He removed me from the battles and the storms on the sea of life. He brought me to a place for training, rest and recuperation. He brought me to the Pink House in the middle of an orange grove.

God, you let me see the wonders of your sanctuary.
Allowed me to delight in the abundance of your storehouse.
You love me and always remain with me. I thank you.
I love and praise you, Your Majesties. Amen!

Adolescent Years

Born in 1941, I grew up during the 1940s and the "happy days" of the 1950's in Sharon with my older brother Bob and sister Arlene in Sharon, Pennsylvania, small town seventy-five miles north of Pittsburgh in western Pennsylvania right on the Ohio border.

Settled in 1795 in a valley on a flat plain along the Shenango River, the community was named after Israel's Plain of Sharon, as depicted in the Bible.

Coal mining was the initial impetus for its growth, but Sharon eventually evolved into steelmaking and then, following the extensive national deindustrialization of the 1970s and '80s through which the city's economy suffered, it slowly rose and diversified. Its economy is now based primarily on light industry, education, healthcare, and social services. The town has survived on its deep core values, built on the solid foundation of family, entrepreneurship, and hard work.

Growing up in this environment, coupled with teachings by example from my large Catholic family, with strong bonds of love, compassion, faith-led Christian values, and a solid work ethic, formed me from an early age. Mom, Dad, my brother, sister and I were all very close. I recall many memorable family activities: vacations by train to New York City, Chicago, and California; car trips to Florida, local parks, picnic outings and visits to relatives every week-end. As thy say, *those were the days my friend, I thought they'd never end.* But they did. My immediate family has since all passed away, including many relatives and friends. My dad and his twelve brothers and sisters grew up in the Flats, so named, the east bank of the river. Each block contained a different Western European nationality. This was where the poorest immigrant families lived in factory houses, all striving for better lives for themselves and their children, built right next to the manufacturing plants that seemed to line the river's shore like a single brick-and-metal-cased, fire-breathing monstrosity that stretched for miles up and down the river stream.

Most boys were destined to stoke the same blast furnaces and work the same pipe mills as their fathers had done and often as their fathers' fathers had done. Sons, uncles, brothers, and cousins, it was not rare to have members of two or three generations working side by side to forge the steel that would help carry the United States through World War II and then into one of the greatest booms in the nation's history.

I still recall the sounds of the steelmaking process: the blast furnaces and the clangs and clanks of rolled steel running through the presses, through which tubes and pipes were being formed. The clicking and whistling sounds heightened late into the evening as we were going to sleep.

Three times a day, year-round, 7:00 a.m., 3:00 p.m., 11:00 p.m. the steel mill's shift whistle signaled and echoed down through the valley and across the entire town, directing the men that it was time for their shift to start or finish their day. Everyone in the town set and rechecked their watches at each whistle blast.

In the 1940s and 1950s, you could hear the railroad switch engines used at the steel mills and the freight and passenger trains stopping day and night for passengers or freight at the station in the middle of downtown. Others were rolling through express from New York City to Chicago and beyond. The New York Central, Pennsylvania, and Erie railroads moved passengers, raw materials, and finished products for thousands of miles east and west from, to, and through the valley. As a young boy, I dreamed of visiting the cities where they traveled.

Many times, I would be awakened in the middle of the night as the house and windows were shaken by louder than normal banging and crashing sounds coming from the mills. The fast-moving molten-steel sheets sometimes buckled, rising rapidly into the air above the roller sets that squeezed the sheets thinner and thinner and then came crashing to the floor. Bells and sirens wailed, and I would look out my second-story bedroom window into the dark and see a red sky illuminated as by a fiery sunset, yet it was from the flames of the nearby blast furnaces. The factories were dangerous places to work.

If you didn't work in the mills, you likely worked at a business that supplied or supported them in some way. Everyone worked. When I entered ninth grade, my mother went to work at the largest department store in town, The Sharon Store (later acquired by the May Department Store Company). She rose through the ranks to become one their head buyers. Mom would travel twice a year on buying trips, spring and fall, to New York City and Chicago. She also was a founding member of the local chapter of the American Business Women's Association. She was president a few times and served on many committees. She was awarded Woman of the Year in 1983.

My parents taught me early to work hard and live right. They provided me a clean home and hot meals every day, but I had to earn my own money for everything else. I was second-generation Italian born in the United States, and I worked many jobs growing up: delivering flowers on holidays, pumping fuel for cars after school and changing oil on weekends, cutting grass in the summer for neighbors, and cleaning up the mud from downtown stores after the annual spring floods. I did whatever I could to make extra money.

I started working when I was six years old. My older brother asked me to be his helper delivering the morning newspaper, seven days a week. When I turned eight, I was given a chance by the local paper distributor to own my own route with twenty-five customers to start. I built it up to 125 in eighteen months by selling door-to-door. When my brother moved on to high school, he gave his route to me and my business doubled overnight. It was my first business merger and acquisition. Each day I rose at 4:00 a.m. when the papers were delivered to the street in front of our house. The truck driver would drop them in large flat bundles tied with twine. Just before driving away, he would look up to my bedroom window and give me a good-morning wave.

I would roll each paper and stuff them into several ink-stained, rain-dampened canvas bags. I would sling them over each of my shoulders and into the front and two rear-side baskets of my older sister's bicycle (we couldn't afford one for me) and pedal off, first delivering to homes on our own street, Service Avenue (a foretelling of my later life's work?).

I rode twenty miles a day, seven days a week, for six years. I couldn't carry all the papers in one load. I had to return to load up the other half. Of necessity I learned logistics, mapping my route for the shortest, fastest, and most efficient use of my time before returning home just before 7:00 a.m. for breakfast, which my mom always had waiting. Then off I would go to St. Joseph's Church for daily Mass at 8:00 a.m., followed by classes at the parish school.

Sundays were the hardest days, because each paper weighed two pounds, twice as much as normal due to the many magazine inserts and coupons for the week ahead. No breakfast this day, though, for when I returned home our entire family would dress in our best clothes for midmorning church service. Then we would go directly to my grandmother's house on my father's side for the rest of the day. All my uncles, aunts, and cousins would be there too. On alternating Sundays, we would visit my grandparents' house on my mother's side. It seemed everyone ate and talked all day long. We played and played. Yes, these were true "happy days."

December and January were the worst months for delivering newspapers. Overnight snow would often pile up to the height of the bike pedals, making it hard to ride, since the snow plows didn't start clearing the streets until 6:00 a.m. The stinging wind made the bitter air even colder, dropping the temperature well below zero for days at a time. On these and rainy days, as a value-added customer service, I placed the papers inside each customer's storm door so they would stay dry and not get wet.

Friday evenings and Saturday mornings (after delivery) were

spent making the rounds again to every customer to collect the week's payments. Thus, I began to learn the nature of business and the many different types of customer personalities. I would carry a few large metal rings with punch cards for each customer listing their name and address (each customer had a duplicate copy). Credit cards did not exist until many years later. I carried a special tool, a hole punch, to punch out the cards as a record that they paid me. It offered a choice of many patterns, and I selected a punch that left a heart-shaped hole in the cards. Appreciative customers often rewarded my service with extra tips. I always had several late payers who would get three or four weeks behind until I stopped delivering to them. They would call the newspaper office and complain that I was skipping them regularly so they would not have to pay. The office was very savvy and kept a record of the deadbeats.

Saturday afternoons, after collecting, I went to the paper distributor's office to pay for my week's papers. I bought the newspapers at a wholesale price, and the difference between the retail price I sold them for left me with a gross profit. Thus, I learned business accounting, collection, and finance. From my gross profits, I paid my administrative expenses. I paid my sister rent for using her bike and the cost of all repairs and tire replacements. What I had I left after this was my net profit, which I gave to my mom, including the tips.

I grossed $15.00 per week. Mom would give me $5.00 as my week's allowance to buy milk at school, a ticket to the movies on Saturday afternoon and popcorn or snacks. This left a balance of $10.00. I paid my sister $3.00 per week rent for using her bike, leaving $7.00 balance. My mother would keep $5.00 for household expenses, leaving a $2.00 balance. This was deposited into my personal bank savings account as a reserve for my sister's bike repairs and tires as needed. My big dream was to save enough in this account to buy my own boy's style bike.

I remember when that day came. One of my happiest childhood days arrived several years later when my dad took me to the bicycle shop and I selected a brand-new, bright, shiny red Schwinn bicycle with whitewall tires, twin chrome handlebar mirrors with red reflectors on the back, a squeeze horn, bell, battery lights front and rear, eighteen-inch-long black-and-white plastic streamers hanging out the end of the handle grips, and bright chrome side and front baskets. Wow! And the best part was I paid cash for it from my paper and odd job savings.

The summer I turned twelve years old, I started working summers for my dad's railroad contracting business. This was after I completed delivering my morning papers. I had to be back home by 7:00 am to get breakfast and leave for work soon after with my dad. If we had a long distance to go, I had to get the paper route done even earlier. My first summer I was the water boy and material helper for the crew repairing and building private railroad spurs into the steel mills and factories. The days were long, hot, and hard.

As the work began, the crew would start singing "Gandy Dancer" song chants, slang for railroad-worker songs, sung by those with heavy Southern African-American accents. This was to coordinate the hard tasks of walking and moving by hand two-hundred-pound, eight-foot-long creosoted wood ties and four-hundred- to six-hundred-pound, thirty-foot-long hot-rolled steel rails, lugging them as far as one hundred yards at a time and hammering spikes in teams of two, alternating hammer blows to the spikes, to secure the rails to the wood ties.

These were strong muscular men, developed from years of railroad work. My dad and the men worked weekdays for the Erie Railroad, doing the same type of work on the main line rail between Cleveland and Pittsburgh. Dad was the crew supervisor. They would tell funny stories about past work incidents during lunch, and we would all laugh. Then when Dad blew his whistle, we would get right back to work. He would blow it in the morning to start work, for a morning and afternoon rest break, lunch, and at end of the day as the sun was setting.

These men were the hardest working, humblest, and kindest I had ever met. They worked seven days a week to provide for their families. I offer high praises to these railroad men of my past and to all others today who labor around the world in all types of physical jobs to earn a living for themselves and their families. Something is to be said for them for they are true salt of the earth.

The second summer I worked for my dad, I placed the spikes in sets on every tie, brought the men drinking water from nearby springs, and bolted the rails together using heavy fishplate couplings. The heavy bolt wrench I used was four feet long to provide leverage and torque in tightening the bolts. In between these tasks, I would fill the rest of my workday shoveling gravel, slag from local iron and steel blast furnaces, and then tamping the stones tight in and around every tie to hold them in place.

When we were building curves, the crew would line up with large crowbars and bend the rails into an arc, holding them in place while others spiked them down. On a good day, we would complete one mile of curved track and two miles of straight track. I wasn't big, but the work made me strong, and in my teen years, I could handle the hardest days relatively easily, eventually working with the crew while singing in chant and carrying the timbers and rails. I never quite got the rhythm of spiking, though, and would watch in awe as those whose trade it was would chant and swing, striking the spike heads split seconds apart until they were driven full deep.

My dad's biceps were as big as most men's thighs from his years of railroad work. When he was younger, each year he would be called to play on the practice squad for the Pittsburgh Steelers. He was asked to go into the mills and find several of the biggest, strongest men and bring them with him on Friday evenings and Saturdays to scrimmage with the team and prepare them for Sunday's competitions. My dad was a sports enthusiast. When he was older, my parents bought a TV. Dad would watch all the major sports, including football, basketball, and baseball. At the same time, he would simultaneously listen to other games on the radio and read the sports section of the newspaper. He knew all the players and their records. He also attended every local high school football and basketball game for years and years. My dad loved his family, work, sports, and politics—stories for another day. I loved my mom and dad.

> **The Secret:** "Those who cultivate their land will have plenty of food, but those who engage in idle pursuits will have plenty of want." (Proverbs 28:19)

> **The Lesson:** Study. Work hard. Develop and live by strong core values. They will guide you in making the best of the many choices life brings you.

Not wanting to live my parents' tough life, upon entering my junior year in high school, I picked classes that would prepare me to go to college as my friends planned to do. But my guidance counselor scoffed when I gave him the list. He then moved very close, inches from my head, his warm breath on my face, which I remember to this day. He said, "Look, son, you're not college material. You're working class, and you're going to work in the mills like the rest of your kind." He then crumpled up my list and threw it in the trash basket. I was stunned.

He proceeded to write a new list of courses for me and told me to sign it. He said there was no use in pretending that I would amount to anything more than a factory worker. This grated on me heavily. I never told my parents or anyone else until many, many years later. To this day, the hair on my neck stands up when I think about it.

I went back to see him again a week later. I was able to convince him to allow me to take some college-prep classes. I wanted to become an engineer. He conceded and agreed only if I also took courses in mechanical drawing (which I greatly enjoyed), metal, wood, and electrical shops. His strong words cut me deeply, and I used them to justify not doing my math homework. Most subjects came very easy to me. I could read my textbooks very quickly and remember most everything after just one time through. I never studied for tests, and I got good grades. But the math was different. One needed to do the homework. I would tell myself, *that counselor is right. I am not cut out for this. I don't want to do the homework. It's too hard.*

Advanced math is only learned by mastering each step at a time as formulas are cumulative. If one step is missed, the wrong answer results. Thus, by not doing my homework, I did not learn certain formulas, and I struggled for grades in algebra, trigonometry, and calculus. I often asked the math teachers to explain why and for what purpose would knowing all these formulas be. They never answered. They just said, "Do the formulas and be quiet!" The result was low math grades. But I did well in languages, getting the highest grades in four years of Latin and advanced English courses.

The summer after I graduated high school, I applied for work in the mills, and they wouldn't hire me. I registered for the military, and they rejected me. This was because I was blind in my right eye. I was born this way, and they said they could not risk injuring my good eye and perhaps totally blinding me for the rest of my life. So all summer long, I thought about what I wanted to do and what would become of me. I wasn't able to toil my life away in the mills and my friends' colleges had rejected me due to my poor grades. Naively, I hadn't even thought about the cost.

One of my part-time jobs was as a golf caddy (golf boy) at the local country club. This gave me a look at how those with wealth lived in their spare time. I knew their homes, all in the high-priced neighborhoods, as I delivered them the morning papers. I saw the fancy cars in their driveways. By the end of the summer, I became determined that I was going to prove that counselor wrong and go to college. I wasn't going to live in a house covered in mill soot forever. I was going to live the life of the country-club set.

College would be the first step to fulfilling my dream. My

parents told me they couldn't pay for me to go, and I certainly couldn't afford to attend any far-flung, prestigious university. Both my financial standing and high school math grades necessitated that I find a school that was close to home so I could commute, saving room-and-board costs. I would need to work full time to pay for my education.

Youngstown State University in Youngstown, Ohio, was that school. When I enrolled it was a private school, and they made their own rules. It was many years later that they became a part of the state's higher education system. It was a forty-minute drive, and they admitted me conditionally on my taking remedial math classes.

I enrolled at Youngstown State in 1959, majoring in civil and mechanical engineering. I had developed a liking for construction by working with my dad and taking mechanical drawing courses in high school. The college required me to retake algebra, trigonometry, and calculus, which I did. This time, I did all my homework and earned high grades. What I learned beyond the formulas was the answer to my question to all my high school teachers —why? Advanced math is the foundation of all engineering disciplines and sciences. I wish they had told me before.

I so enjoyed my newfound freedom my first semester at college that I spent it skipping classes and goofing off. As a result, my train ran off the track. Other than my math classes I skipped mandatory orientation, physical education, voluntary ROTC, and others. It was also during this time that I spotted in the college's cafeteria the most beautiful girl I had ever seen, and she happened to be a close friend of my cousin. I recall vividly she was wearing a green-plaid jumper skirt with a white blouse, her blond, reddish hair worn pulled back in a ponytail with forehead bangs and hazel eyes that changed color it seemed. Yes, it was my wife-to-be, the love of my life, Paula.

We started dating, attending formally dressed school dances. I wore my ROTC uniform, and Paula wore beautiful gowns and one-of-a-kind dresses. She soon settled me down, we married a year later, and she put my train back on the track. I decided I did not want to be using formulas for the rest of my life, and I changed my major to business. I scored 4.0s in all my classes. I was asked to join the honorary business fraternity due to my high grades, and I was elected treasurer and a member of the executive committee.

I eventually squeezed a four-year degree into seven years, graduating with high honors and a bachelor of science degree in industrial marketing with minors in accounting and business organization. Accounting came very easy to me, having learned the discipline of advanced mathematics, so much so, that the head accounting professor encouraged me to pursue accounting as a career.

During those years, I worked full-time as a bartender, six nights a week, to pay for my schooling as well as provide for my new family. Working through college as a young father, I learned to set priorities, meet deadlines, and balance time between work and school, which involved writing a multitude of class papers. Sundays were always reserved for church and family. But school and work took the dominant portion of my life. This became a habit and would help me later in life to climb the corporate ladder to the success that I envisioned and so craved. Three of our children were in the audience when I walked to receive my college diploma.

GPS: Guiding Principles to Success

I learned to follow the world's GPS system—guiding principles to success. These led me to the accumulation of wealth, power and prestige, eventually owning several homes, condos, boats, cars, country-club memberships, and artifacts. I jetted across the country on private planes, working for big corporations, entertaining clients at sporting events, and dining in fine restaurants. I was successful by the world's standard definition of success during my twenties to forties.

The Secret: "The God of this age has blinded the minds of the unbelievers, so that they may not see the light of the gospel." (2 Corinthians 4:4)

The Lesson: By the time I reached my fifties, I realized there's more to life than the climb.

Many values taught by the world conflict with the core values taught in the Bible. Scriptural virtues such as humility, kindness, and respect for others versus hubris—to live simply instead of seeking power, status, and prestige; generosity instead of hoarding; self-control instead of self-indulgence; and forgiveness instead of revenge.

For many years the pursuit of fame and fortune fed my ego but created large blind spots in my thinking and set me on a ship adrift in the saltwater sea of life. Just as winds are needed to stress trees as they grow so they become strong, bend, and resist toppling by the power of heavy storms, we, as well, must encounter daily winds of change and strife for our core values to be developed and become strong so we can resist toppling when the heavy storms of life pound on us. While sailing among the islands of success on the saltwater sea of life, I landed and climbed to the summits of the mountain islands of pride, power, and prestige, but I kept encountering violent storms that challenged my abilities to command the ship. My core values were often tested: just say yes and sail on to new riches and perhaps become admiral of the fleet, or choose to say no and be marooned while the ship sails off without you, or so I thought.

When I made that pivotal decision to not take riches and resigned, I went into a lifeboat in the midst of the storm. Tossed about, I shipwrecked and washed ashore on the rocks of Safety Harbor, Florida. There I wandered into the valley of despair. I pleaded for help, and I was rescued and given a place to rest and recover. There I discovered a new adventure to pursue, like Ponce De Leon who adventurously sought the Fountain of Youth. An ocean of saltwater had failed to quench my thirst, so I now sought life's purpose and peace instead. I found that thirst-quenching Holy Water in an orange grove next to a cracker bungalow. I found it at the Pink House.

> **The Secret:** "I will instruct you and show you the way you should walk, give you counsel with my eye upon you." (Psalm 32:8)

> **The Lesson:** Abide with the Lord.

Abiding: The loving, gentle, caring, willing unifying of self-will with God's will, melding our spiritual heart with God's Spirit. Do not think of it in terms of a "hostile takeover." Spiritual Surrender is not crushing humiliation. It is a time of celebration! Like a caterpillar struggles then morphs into a butterfly, spiritual transformation is a struggle and leads one to morph into a new life in Christ. Your spiritual eye will be opened to see what God see's. He will provide you enlightenment, instruction, counsel, guidance, purpose, direction and protection.

> **The Secret**: "Jesus advanced [in] wisdom and age and favor before God and man." (Luke 2:52)

One morning after I read this Bible verse I began to think about its meaning as I walked through the orange grove. I thought, *Well, the Bible provides guidance on how to live a full life.* Like Paul, the Apostle, I longed to learn to be contented in all good and bad circumstances.

I concluded that moderation in all things, balance and simplification are key. Here I was in this orange grove, broke, living in the Pink House, the good life (many possessions) I'd once had was gone.

I was amazed how the words of scripture now were becoming so clear. It was a new beginning to a deeper understanding of the meaning of life. The words were as though they were backlit with a brilliant light. In time, instead of reading a whole chapter or several verses at one time, I would read but one short phrase or verse and then stop and deeply reflect on its meaning. I began to grasp insights never before realized. I was being spiritually enlightened. I was learning to navigate by God's GPS system instead of the world's.

GPS: God's Principles to Success

The Lesson: Practice living a balanced life by using GPS—God's principles for success.

1. He advanced in *wisdom*. We are to advance *intellectually*, in knowledge, understanding, and discernment.
2. He advanced in *age*. We are to advance *physically*, maintaining our bodies by proper exercise, food and rest.
3. He advanced in *favor before God*. We are to advance *spiritually*.
4. He advanced in *favor before man*. We are to advance in *social-emotional* development.

Neglect to develop any of these four attributes, and like a four-legged stool, if one or more legs are short, we are unbalanced and may topple over. We each grow differently and mature at different times and speeds. Do not compare yourself to others. Create a personal balance scorecard and every week reflect on how well you advanced. Better yet, if you really wish to stay focused, do so every day at noon and in the evening. Score yourself on each of these four attributes on a scale of one to five (highest). What did you do well? What did you do OK? What did you do poorly or not at all? Are you committed? Are you willing? What action are you going to take today? Then calibrate yourself and go do it! As you do these each day you will slowly become balanced and discover a remarkable inner peace an advance up the invisible spiral ramp.

Wisdom—Intellectual Development
1. Increase your knowledge, experience, understanding, and discernment.
   - Develop common sense, and insight.
   - Multidimensionally think and act using reason over emotional reactions.
2. Develop a deep understanding of people, objects, events, situations, and
   - The willingness as well as
   - The ability to apply your perception, judgment, and
   - Take the optimal course of action in given circumstances.

Age—Physical Development
1. Moderate daily food intake.
2. Take daily exercise.
3. Ensure daily rest.

Favor before God—Spiritual Development: The neighborhood fitness center where I occasionally work out is filled with men and women of all ages building better bodies. I watch them push themselves on the treadmills and machines. Some take bodybuilding supplements to advance their muscle strength. Some do extended cardio to strengthen their hearts. Others just tone and maintain. Some are overweight and weak; others look lean and strong. I wonder at times if they are strengthening their spiritual hearts as well. Only God knows.

Spiritual transformation is like bodybuilding in that it is not instantaneous. Paul remained in Damascus for some time after his dramatic enlightenment, during which he strengthened his spiritual heart. This is no overnight change, and it does not happen by repeating a Bible verse here and there or skimming through a passage. No, it calls for *soaking* yourself in the scriptures until the Holy Spirit connects with your spirit and produces the nature and ways of Christ in you. Jesus said, "If you remain in me and my words remain in you, [abide] ask for whatever you want and it will be done for you." God's training is designed to grow us in favor with Him.

> **The Secret:** "Train yourself for devotion, for, while physical training is of limited value, devotion is valuable in every respect, since it holds a promise of life both for the present and for the future." (1 Timothy 4:7–8)

> **The Lesson:** Work out frequently to develop your spiritual heart.

We strengthen and tone the soul through grace, which comes with knowledge, understanding, and discernment of the Word of God. Keeping our spiritual hearts strong and fit must be our first priorities, the one things we do above all others.

The heart is a muscle—the muscle that keeps the other muscles going. It's good to build and tone our other muscles, but the essential thing, the first priority, is doing whatever keeps both the physical and spiritual heart strong.

Favor before Man—Social / Emotional Development:
1. Form and sustain positive relationships.
2. Understand, manage, and express your emotions.
3. Explore and engage with others in your environments.
4. Express your ideas and feelings.
5. Display empathy toward others.
6. Manage your feelings of frustration and disappointment.
7. Feel self-confident.
8. Develop friendships.
9. Be humble.
10. Work hard.
11. Be emotionally smart.

God used my time in the Pink House to instruct and mature me, as He had used the desert to teach and prepare the nation of Israel for their successful entry into their Promised Land. When they were leaving Egypt, the Lord led them to take the long wilderness road instead of the short coastal road. I too wondered daily where God was leading me, when would I get there, and what I would do, but if I had continued to take the easy road, no doubt it would have led to endless disaster. Instead, God took me to my desert oasis near the crossroads of Patience and Destiny. The path through the orange grove at the Pink House led me to discover the well of Holy Water and prepared me for a new life in my promised land.

CHAPTER 3
Chameleon

Wealth is a Gift received from the Lord.
Otherwise, you might say in your heart,
"It is my own power and the strength of my
own hand that has got me this wealth."
(Deuteronomy 8:17)

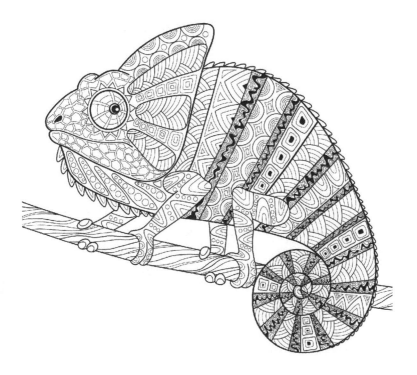

May 1966, I graduated from Youngstown State University and started my business career at Westinghouse Electric Corporation's world headquarters in Pittsburgh, Pennsylvania. Founded in 1886 and employing 120,000 in 1968, with $2 billion dollars in sales, Westinghouse Electric Corporation was among the country's largest electronics companies, with units committed to serving the US defense industry, as well as interests in power generation, vertical transportation (elevators and escalators), and manufacturing. The company also maintained an office furniture subsidiary, The Knoll Group, and a broadcasting subsidiary, Westinghouse Broadcasting.

I was hired into the conglomerate's Management Development Department and introduced to fellow college graduates. Except for me, they were all from big-name schools: Harvard, Yale, MIT, Cornell, Columbia, and others. They came from the homes of the privileged and wealthy. Their schooling had been paid for, and most of them had never worked in their life. I had worked since I was six years old, and I paid all my own education costs. I had also squeezed a four-year program into seven years. I was grateful for having been selected to join this group, but at the same time I felt envious and somewhat intimidated. I resolved to prove my worth.

> **The Secret:** "Be doers of the word and not hearers only, deluding yourselves. For if anyone is a hearer of the word and not a doer, he is like a man who looks at his own face in a mirror. He sees himself, then goes off and promptly forgets what he looked like. But the one who peers into the perfect law* of freedom and perseveres, and is not a hearer who forgets but a doer who acts, such a one shall be blessed in what he does." (James 1:22–25)
>
> **The Lesson:** Take action—Do it! It is not what you own, where you're from or what you say, but what you do in obedience to the will of God. "Not

everyone who says to me, 'Lord, Lord,' will enter
the kingdom of heaven, but only the one who does
the will of my Father in heaven." (Matthew 7:21)

Do not be anyone with regret at the end of life saying, "I coulda,
woulda, shoulda." Be someone who says, "I did it." And our Father
will say, "Well done!"

> "Inaction breeds doubt and fear. Action breeds
> confidence and courage. If you want to conquer
> fear, do not sit home and think about it. Go out and
> get busy."—Dale Carnegie

I took Dale Carnegie's advice and set out at once to get things
done. The people of Westinghouse's Corporate Management
Development staff were subject matter experts. Each highly
knowledgeable in specialized areas. They taught us in daily classes,
using their past consulting work within the corporation as case
study examples. It was just like attending an advanced MBA business
school. Mornings, we were in class, and afternoons, we worked
on assignments. Weekly guest lecturers would come, presidents,
senior vice presidents, and high-level managers of various business
units. They presented their business issues, strategies, operational
plans, and quarterly results. They would present critical problems
and then ask us for our recommendations. This was followed by a
general question-and-answer session.

We attended "charm school". We were taught business manners
and etiquette like how to select conservative business clothes,
proper grooming, and how to entertain clients. Monthly they
would take us to exclusive, private business clubs for luncheons
and to fine-dining restaurants for seven-course evening meals with
senior executives. We were instructed to taste our food before
adding salt or pepper, keep elbows off the table, put hands in our
laps, the order in which to use tableware and glasses, and what price

range food and types of cocktails to order. Wine experts conducted tastings and taught us how to select reds and whites based on the customer's choice of meal. We also learned proper toasting for praising the dinner guests.

The first six months at Westinghouse, I was assigned case work, assisting the management consultants as an intern on projects in a variety of business divisions. This provided me the opportunity to meet and learn about the division's people, their daily work routines, products, distribution, and all facets of their business. It provided the operation managers the opportunity to get to know us graduates and decide whether to offer us permanent positions.

One of my last assignments was to the Engineering Department of the Elevator and Escalator Division. This unit held the largest market share for their products in the United States and ranked second globally. I was soon offered a permanent position as a management trainee, which I accepted, earning a salary of $600.00 a month plus benefits, a large pay increase over my first job delivering newspapers at $60.00 a month before expenses.

For the next six months, I reviewed construction contract terms and conditions, the fine print, learning legal terminology, meanings, and risks. The next six months, I focused on learning scope of work and engineering specification details, reviewing architect and engineering blueprint drawings, and I went on factory tours.

After a year of mastering the legal and technical aspects of the business, I was promoted to a sales engineer position and assigned to the district office in downtown Pittsburgh. Unlike other sales engineers who worked in one department only, I was assigned to two. The first was the new construction department, and the second was the maintenance, repair, and modernization department. They explained it as "matrix management," and I was to report directly to the two separate department managers. This was difficult as these two managers were always in competition with each other to impress their superiors, and I was their pawn being directed this way and that.

The Secret: "No one can serve two masters. He will either hate one and love the other, or be devoted to one and despise the other. You cannot serve God and mammon." (Matthew 6:24)

The Lesson: No one can serve two masters. He will either hate one and love the other, or be devoted to one and despise the other. You cannot serve God and mammon." (Matthew 6:24)

Despite the struggle, the good news was I excelled in both arenas and learned the practical application of selling and engineering vertical transportation systems for high-rise buildings. Experiencing first hand maintenance, repair, and modernization projects taught me not to overspecify or underspecify new construction, as both extremes resulted in unhappy long-term customers. If a building was built with the equipment systems in place but not correctly engineered, users would be upset, and it would cost hundreds of thousands of dollars to change.

Having learned the results of equipment wear and building life cycles, I had a personal competitive knowledge advantage in consulting with architects and engineers in writing equipment specifications for both new and remodeled high-rise buildings, shopping malls, and sport stadiums. I learned tiered-organization selling as numerous influencers and decision makers were involved in these multimillion-dollar projects: owners, developers, architects, engineers, general contractors, banks, property managers, and regulators. I flourished in this environment, consistently placing in the company's top sales producer rankings. I was recognized several times, receiving the highest corporate award, the President's Circle, among many others. The company continued grooming me for upper management. They sent me annually to the University of Virginia Darden School of Business, where I took courses in finance, executive leadership, and organization management. I was also selected to attend the annual stockholders' meetings with the board of directors. I recall while still in my early thirties being at a dinner before a meeting. I was seated at a table with Henry Ford II on one side of me and Donald Burnham, CEO, on the other.

I was quickly and repeatedly promoted to positions of increasing responsibility, transferring from Pittsburgh to New York City to Miami to Indianapolis. I was in charge of three states at the age of thirty. The first year, I personally sold absolutely nothing, and I was disillusioned. Transferred from big-city successes to Indianapolis or "Indian-no-place," I was a newcomer to town. I joined the Rotary Club, several other business groups, and the prestigious Indianapolis Athletic Club. There I became acquainted with the movers and shakers, the decision makers of the city and state.

> **The Secret:** "Trust in the LORD and do good that you may dwell in the land and live secure. Find your delight in the LORD who will give you your heart's desire." (Psalm 37:3–4)

> **The Lesson:** Creating trust is critical in developing relationships.

The second year I was there, our three-state team took first place in the United States, growing from the company's last-place ranking for each of the past ten years. We repeated and held first place for the next few years. Employee count grew from six to one hundred and fifty in Indianapolis alone. I was the youngest district manager in the company and full of myself.

The office furniture market was now booming in the mid-1970s as the cubicle culture took hold, and Westinghouse was at the forefront. They promoted me in 1975 and moved our family to Grand Rapids, Michigan, home of their furniture headquarters and factory. I was now manager in charge of five Midwest states. Again, it was the company's lowest-ranked region. I put a new team in place and took it to first place, holding top ranking again for several years in a row.

Then it happened. I was totally blindsided. A company announcement creating a new position was issued, naming a peer manager from Chicago to oversee all sales. Me and five other regional managers now reported directly to him.

I confronted my boss, asking how long this was in the planning and why I wasn't selected. He told me his boss planned it. But my boss originally was from Chicago and worked for years together with the new guy. He had known it was in the works for a while, because when I asked when would the Chicago guy be in the office, he said, "Tomorrow, the moving van left yesterday."

It was hard for me to take. Paula and I had become, what I believed to be, very close friends with my boss. Our homes were only a block apart, and we went out to dinner together every week. Their two children were in the same school and grades as two of our children. Paula and the bosses wife also got together several times a week. They never once hinted a management change was coming.

I was disappointed, angry, envious, and full of hubris. It would take me months to overcome these hard feelings. My boss tried to justify the move. He said the manager moving up from Chicago was a career furniture-industry guy, while I was career corporate. He would not go any further up the ladder, while I had a very bright future and was fifteen years younger. My mind was closed by pride, and I would not listen. I told him I was going to look for another job.

Surprisingly, within a few days, they promoted me, creating a new position of equal rank, placing me in charge of what they called national specialty sales. I was given complete freedom in creating the business plan and recruiting my team, no doubt as they had no plan in mind at the time. Somewhat soothed, my competitive spirit kicked in. I designed an approach that increased annual revenues from $17 million to $125 million within four years. Every year, our team contributed the greatest percentage of sales, dwarfing general sales. We developed market niches and specialized dealers for our removable floor-to-ceiling walls and raised computer flooring, which elevated the floor surface by 14 inches to accommodate the placement of large amounts of cable wiring connecting mainframe computers to our cubicle workstations as the computer age was born. We created and developed a corporate national account program, recruited top senior sales specialists from around the country and assigned them to vertical industry markets such as banking, electronics, automotive, heavy and light manufacturing, all within the Fortune 500s and targeted federal and state governments.

After long discussions with Paula about the situation, though, and how we felt betrayed, I just could not overcome my feelings of being humiliated when I was told I must report to the guy from Chicago. I brooded privately, biding my time until I reached my fifteen-year employment anniversary. At that point, my retirement pension would be fully vested, and I would be free to leave Westinghouse. Several large corporations were headquartered in Western Michigan, and this would allow me to get off the moving train to promotions, complete my business career, and allow our children to finish schooling.

Soon after a large office furniture manufacturer, Herman Miller, offered me a career position, and I gave notice at Westinghouse. This was when my boss finally apologized for the past situation and quickly countered with a matching raise in pay. I declined and told him how hurt I was over the moves they had made. I just could not get over it. He tried to again convince me to stay, saying I was corporate, and future moves were coming. A few days later, he countered again and said a position was available as vice president of marketing and sales with Westinghouse's commercial air conditioning business headquartered in Boston. I asked if that would be my last stop and was told no. If I accepted and performed well, which he said my track record indicated I would, I would be named president of this business and eventually transferred back to the world headquarters in Pittsburgh.

By this time, Paula had wearied of long-distant moves, and we thought our four children must have stability in their schooling and friends as well as for ourselves. We had developed close relationships with other couples, and we were very comfortable living in western Michigan. I accepted Herman Miller's offer, and within a few months I was named director of marketing for the United States and based at their world headquarters in Zeeland, Michigan. I believed my long-term career future was cemented.

It was a short twenty-minute drive from our Grand Rapids home, and it allowed our children to stay in the same school system. Herman Miller suited my ambition well, because it was the leading nationally known brand, innovative, entrepreneurial, and a high-end commercial interior furnishings manufacturer. The environment was perfect for my style of bold, inspiring leadership. The team and programs I put in place helped our salespeople increase annual revenues from $350 million to $500 million within four years. During this time, I continued my education and earned a master's in management degree from Aquinas College.

Unfortunately, a few years later the vice president who had recruited me was swept out in a corporate restructuring when a new president was hired. Herman Miller was a publicly held stock company, and its board of directors responded to shareholders' demands for higher money distributions and replaced the president. I was let go along with many other senior managers.

> **The Secret**: "Its leaders render judgment for a bribe, the priests teach for pay, the prophets divine for money, while they rely on the LORD, saying, "Is not the LORD in the midst of us? No evil can come upon us!" (Micah 3:11)

> **The Lesson**: "Better to take refuge in the LORD than to put one's trust in mortals. Better to take refuge in the LORD than to put one's trust in princes." (Psalm 118: 8–9)

Released in 2010, the movie *The Company Men* accurately depicts what terrible turmoil, emotionally and economically, is created in the lives of those let go when corporate downsizing of the workforce takes place. I personally experienced this roller coaster of depressive emotions and family disruption and witnessed community devastation, having been fired from Herman Miller and growing up in western Pennsylvania during the time it was the world center of the iron and steel manufacturing industry, now known as the rust belt.

I spent many a night in the basement on my knees, praying for God to help me find work so I could support my wife and four children, three of them now in college.

Lord, Grant us the candor to admit to each other that sometimes life overwhelms us. And grant us the courage to help others find help—and to seek it when we need it. Hope comes with help from God and others. Amen! Your will be done.
—Jack Manilla

After much personal resistance to tell others of my job loss, due to my hubris, I finally shared my dilemma. I told an industry associate that I could not find work and was desperate. He quickly referred me to a privately held, midsize Steelcase office interiors dealer, and after several months of dead-end job searching, on the very day not one penny was left in our bank account, I received a job offer in New York City. I was immensely grateful for this opportunity and fell to my knees in thanksgiving to my Lord.

The Secret: "Your Father knows what you need before you ask him." (Matthew 6:8)

The Lesson: "There is an appointed time for everything, and a time for every affair under the heavens … God has made everything appropriate to its time." (Ecclesiastes 3:1, 11)

Though much smaller than the large manufacturing companies to which I had become accustomed, they offered me greater freedom, responsibility, and "psychic income" as vice president marketing and sales. Additionally, I functioned as senior project executive overseeing installations for prestigious corporate headquarters such as those of AT&T, BMW USA, Volvo USA, Sharp Electronics USA, and Nextel. Working with these business behemoths stroked my ego, filling me with power and prestige. However, I was back working in a matrix-management structure. The business was owned by two partners, each holding 50 percent share. One was very B2B (business-to-business) commercially oriented, the other B2C (business-to-consumer) retail oriented. As a result, a constant tug of war existed between them, and again I was the pawn in the middle.

The B2B owner brought in his two sons when they graduated college. The other owner did the same with one son. All three were assigned to report to me, and I was given the responsibility to groom and teach them the business. After eight years of substantial profitable growth both owners/fathers retired and placed the three sons in charge of everything. My ego grated heavily under this arrangement. I had been promised when hired that I would "be well taken care of" when it came time for the owners to retire. I confronted the owners on this, and they said, "It is what it is."

> **The Secret:** "Better to take refuge in the LORD than
> to put one's trust in mortals. Better to take refuge
> in the LORD than to put one's trust in princes."
> (Psalm 118: 8–9)

> **The Lesson:** "I'm not upset that you lied to me.
> I'm upset that from now on I can't believe you."
> (Friedrich Nietzsche)

Word around the industry soon was out, and an executive recruiter contacted me on hearing of the owner and management changes where I worked. He encouraged me to meet with his client who was searching for someone with my skills. Still yearning for more glory, I left in sixty days to join another Steelcase dealer in Milford, Connecticut, as executive vice president/general manager with stock bonuses. This was a profit-turnaround situation. It required much work, but the reward would be significant wealth. Accustomed to the former, and ever longing for the latter, I immersed myself in the challenge, working one hundred hours a week. I assessed the business and implemented a plan. I consolidated responsibilities, reduced staff and management positions, and closed a satellite office in Greenwich, Connecticut. I replaced salespeople and sales managers and initiated performance-based incentives that increased sales volume and margins. Company profits rose quickly, and in less than one year the business was turned around.

On the anniversary of my joining this firm, the owner came to my office, and I anticipated a large reward. He congratulated me on a job well done and announced he had sold the business. When I asked the him about my stock bonus, he replied simply, "The corporation no longer exists. Our deal is null and void."

I was then introduced to the new owner. I was pleased with his professionalism, and he reminded me of the senior managers I had worked with at Westinghouse. I was assigned to report to his vice president located in their home office in Hartford, Connecticut. He asked me to spend a day with him, driving into New York City for business meetings. Well, after spending a full day with him, I knew it would not work out between us. I immediately began a new job search, letting my industry contacts know I was looking for a new position. I was lost again on the sea of life, searching for another island of success. I had to learn this Secret and Lesson once again.

> **The Secret** (repeated): "Better to take refuge in the
> Lord than to put one's trust in mortals. Better to
> take refuge in the Lord than to put one's trust in
> princes." (Psalm 118:8–9)

The Lesson (repeated): I'm not upset that you lied to me. I'm upset that from now on I can't believe you." (Friedrich Nietzsche)

True to form, within thirty days I found a similar business in Florida that carried the Haworth Furniture line and joined as executive vice president. This time I secured an employment contract in writing covering all contingencies. I assembled a dynamic team of twenty-plus salespeople. Having personally worked for the three largest industry competitors, Westinghouse (now Knoll), Herman Miller, and Steelcase, I knew their weaknesses and struck the right business value proposition, propelling us to grow fourfold. Doubling sales every year, our team went from $7 million in annual sales to $20 million in a few short years.

Now in my early fifties, I had finally seemed to fulfill my worldly dreams. We were living very comfortably, thanks to my hard-earned success. But our dream was soon to become another nightmare.

CHAPTER 4
Choices

"Train yourself for devotion, while physical training is of limited value, devotion is valuable in every respect, since it holds a promise of life both for the present and for the future."
(1 Timothy 4:7)

Life was good in Florida. We were comfortable in our newly renovated pool home in a gated golf-course community with our bank account filling and my ego swelling. Contented, I desired nothing more—except more and more and more. Then it happened.

I gave it little thought at first. The company was thriving, thanks largely to my business skills, and my reputation was stellar. I was as honest and reputable as an executive could be, so there was no reason to suspect that something may be amiss.

It started innocently. Employees came to me saying there was something wrong with their commission statements. Paying little heed, I kept telling them to work it out with the accounting department. This went on and on for a few months, and when I kept mentioning it to my senior partner, he simply said, "There's no problem. They're mistaken."

It was our daily habit to discuss business over morning coffee in his large, corner, windowed office. We were sitting on leather side chairs next to the sofa. The room had a conference table, bookcases, and desk— all done in traditional classic mahogany. When he finished his coffee, he got up and closed the door. He then walked over, patted me on the back, and congratulated me on what a great job I was doing.

He said, "I'm going to cut you in for a big piece of the action."

Thrilled, I thanked him and asked, "What does that mean?"

He said, "You're going to get a large share of stock in the business."

"That's wonderful," I said, beaming and thinking of how I couldn't wait to tell Paula.

He patted me on the back again and said, "I've also got a big bonus check ready for you."

Ecstatic, I was smiling from ear to ear.

I finished my coffee, stood up, thanked him for the recognition, and shook his hand as he sat behind his desk.

I walked to the door, grasped the handle, and just as I was about to open it, he said, "Oh, by the way, there's one more thing."

I stopped and turned around. The moment was just like that in the old TV detective show *Columbo* when he's on the way out of a room, stops, turns and says, "Oh, one more thing."

The Secret: "Then the devil took him up to a very high mountain, and showed him all the kingdoms of the world in their magnificence, and he said to him, 'All these I shall give to you, if you will prostrate yourself and worship me.'" (Matthew 4:8–9)

There was an awkward silent moment as I walked over to his desk. I waited for him to speak.

He said, "You'll have to keep your mouth shut about the commissions."

I replied, "What?"

He admitted he was keeping two sets of books and cheating the employees out of their commissions. He said he was adding bogus costs to the sales orders. He said again, "Keep your mouth shut, and I'll cut you in for a big piece of the action."

In the next instant, I resigned and walked out.

The Lesson: "At this, Jesus said to him, 'Get away, Satan! It is written" (Deuteronomy 6:13–15),

"The Lord, your God, shall you worship and him alone shall you serve." (Matthew 4:10)

And "Then he said to the crowd, "Take care to guard against all greed, for though one may be rich, one's life does not consist of possessions." (Luke 12:15)

We make choices every day in our personal, family, and business lives. Right choices in the small, simple stuff prepares us to make right choices in the big stuff.

> **The Secret:** "The person who is trustworthy in very small matters is also trustworthy in great ones; and the person who is dishonest in very small matters is also dishonest in great ones. If, therefore, you are not trustworthy with dishonest wealth, who will trust you with true wealth? If you are not trustworthy with what belongs to another, who will give you what is yours?" (Luke 16:10–12)

> **The Lesson**: Do the right things and do things right. "So for one who knows the right thing to do and does not do it, it is a sin." (James 4:17)

When it comes to the big choices like the one offered to me, it would have been easy to avoid confrontation with the perpetrator and my core values by glossing over, minimizing, or rationalizing the importance of honesty and integrity. After all, a fortune was at hand. In today's world of declining values, it becomes easier and easier to ignore the fact that something is wrong by making certain choices and justify self-satisfying choices. *We deserve it,* we tell ourselves. *We've earned it. The fortune is there for us to take. Think of all the things money can buy. Go for it!*

All our lives we are involved in a personal civil war. Even after spiritual transformation. I often thought about this as the years passed. Why, after experiencing the miracle in the mist, the journey through the orange grove, the Pink House experiences, and making all the right choices. did I still have these battles?

Then one day the secret was revealed. The apostle Paul, years after his dramatic experience on the road to Damascus when he was struck as by lightning, his transformation and his years of ministry, had written it in his letters to the Romans and the Galatians.

> **The Secret:** "We know that the law is spiritual; but I am carnal, sold into slavery to sin. What I do, I do

not understand. For I do not do what I want, but I do what I hate." (Romans 7:14–15)

We want to do right, but we do wrong. We are split personalities. One never knows when these major battles will come. We fight these battles alone in the shadows of our minds. We know we need and should be prepared to make right decisions. Is the choice going to result in a short-term life of temporal gain here on Earth? Or will we make a life-changing choice for everlasting happiness in the great eternity? It depends on the strength of our values, our core beliefs, and if we are faith-led.

Even after we are spiritually transformed, we still will make wrong choices because we are human and our old nature always remains. You can still lose your temper and make hurtful remarks. Tempting thoughts of all sorts still creep into your mind.

The Lesson: "I say, then: live by the Spirit and you will certainly not gratify the desire of the flesh. For the flesh has desires against the Spirit, and the Spirit against the flesh; these are opposed to each other." (Galatians 5:16)

When these battles come remember to call for help, a supernatural spiritual air strike.

"Lord, we are about to be overwhelmed by the enemy. I can't win on my own. Send help!"

The Lesson: "As long as Moses kept his hands raised up, Israel had the better of the fight, but when he let his hands rest, Amalek had the better of the fight. Moses' hands grew tired; so they took a rock and put it under him and he sat on it. Meanwhile Aaron and Hur supported his hands, one on one side and one on the other, so that his hands remained steady until sunset. And Joshua defeated Amalek and his people with the sword." (Exodus 17:11–13)

I made a life-changing decision the day I rejected the offer of riches. When I did, I was at complete peace and comfortable with the decision. I knew I had made the right choice when soon after a feeling of great calm and warmth enveloped me. I felt a freedom like never before. Little did I know something else was about to happen.

The net result of that one decision was the Lord stripped me of all the material goods that I had acquired in a lifetime. Cash, homes, condominiums, boats, cars, all my toys were taken away and we moved into a cracker-box bungalow, the Pink House, and I walked through the orange grove each morning and afternoon, pointing to the clouds, angrily shaking my fist and saying, "Lord, I did the right thing. Why am I being punished?"

It took a while until I came to realize I wasn't being punished: I was being tested and taught lessons. The first lesson I had to learn was that while all things come from God. God will give and God will take.

> **The Secret**: "Yours are the heavens, yours the earth; you founded the world and everything in it." (Psalms 89:12)

> **The Lesson**: "In all circumstances give thanks. for this is the will of God for you in Christ Jesus." (1 Thessalonians 5:18)

After two-thirds of my life, I thought that I was living a right life in accordance with the simple basic rules that were established thousands of years ago and that we can still find today in the Old Testament. They're called the Ten Commandments. I had never killed anyone, and I was not a terrorist, but I wasn't Mother Teresa either. I like to think I fit this description.

"Being a male is a matter of birth. Being a man is a matter of age. But being a gentleman is a matter of choice."
(Mark Sinclair, aka Vin Diesel)

The Secret: "But when you pray, go to your inner room, close the door, and pray to your Father in secret." (Matthew 6:6)

The Lesson: "And your Father who sees in secret will repay you. In praying, do not babble like the pagans, who think that they will be heard because of their many words ... Do not be like them. Your Father knows what you need before you ask him." (Matthew 6:7–8)

The next lesson came to me when I read and reflected on the Ten Commandments and what they meant to me. The first commandment is to love God with all your heart and all your soul. I realized I had rationalized my pursuit of materialism and had put God second in my life. When I came to this conviction, I was awestruck. I had created a blind spot in my mind. It hit me like a piece of two-by-four lumber on my head. I literally fell to my knees in the orange grove and apologized aloud, "God, I am so sincerely sorry. Please forgive me." It took the removal of all wealth to get my attention.

The Secret: "Teacher, which commandment in the law is the greatest?" He said to him, "You shall love the Lord, your God, with all your heart, with all your soul, and with all your mind. This is the greatest and the first commandment. The second is like it: You shall love your neighbor as yourself. The whole law and the prophets depend on these two commandments." (Matthew 22:36–40)

The Lesson: Pause and reflect daily to answer these questions: How did I do yesterday? Did I put God first in everything?

After this realization at the Pink House, I began this self-evaluation practice and continue doing so to this day. I am human and still do not do what I wish to do all the time, but I am getting better about remembering to apologize to others and to God when I do.

I contemplate daily Bible readings and devotional reflections, personalizing their meanings as I reflect on how they relate directly to me. I have developed the habit of reading just one or two verses. I find each word contains precious jewels of knowledge that I would have missed if I read on and on. One spoon at a time, tasting and swirling, has so much more enjoyment than trying to take in too much at one time. I also began keeping a daily journal of my thoughts at the Pink House, which I share with you now.

These personal reflections allowed me to discover deeper understandings of God's word, and I got to know myself much better. The experience was, and is, as though God was talking to me directly as in conversation. Now when I hear others read and quote scripture I become frustrated when they cover an entire page. So much is being missed.

I also learned to practice being patient, to meditate, to contemplate, and to listen to the beauty of silence, while abiding with God. I found answers to questions I never asked of myself before when I quieted my mind and opened my heart and soul.

In time, all on my own, I developed a prayer practice, a five-step process.

1. Thanks, and Praise
2. Scripture Reading
3. Meditation/Contemplation
4. Personal Reflection
5. Journaling

Years later when I was on retreat at the Monastery of the Holy Spirit in Conyers, Georgia, while sharing with a spiritual advisor, one of the monks, he told me God had self-enlightened me and gave a name for this practice that has been used for centuries. In Latin, it is called *Lectio Divina* ("from the Divine"). I was greatly encouraged when I learned that Pope Francis follows this same process daily.

Since my days at the Pink House, I have continued to pray this way every morning. It has become a joy, so much so that I rise easily from sleep each day in the predawn, anxious to visit with "We Am" (God the Father, the Son, and the Holy Spirit), the angels, and the saints. I first go for a thirty-minute walk before the sun rises, thanking and praising the Lord as dawn breaks and the sun rises. My thoughts often drift to the prior day and all the tasks for the day at hand. I have to tell myself there is time enough later for these. This time is reserved for prayer and abiding with God.

On return to the house I settle into my "inner room" with a cup of fresh coffee, the Bible, journal, daily devotionals, and a spiritual book or two. There the angels always have a seat saved for me with my friends at the spiritual breakfast table. There the holy ones welcome us, anxiously waiting to visit and share knowledge, understanding, and discernment. God the Father called Abraham and Jacob friend and invites us each to be friend as well. "But you, Israel, my servant, Jacob, whom I have chosen, offspring of Abraham my friend" (Isaiah 41:8).

> **The Secret**: "But you, man of God, avoid all this. Instead, pursue righteousness, devotion, faith, love, patience, and gentleness. Compete well for the faith. Lay hold of eternal life, to which you were called when you made the noble confession in the presence of many witnesses." (1 Timothy 6:6–12)

> **The Lesson**: Willingness. When I willingly chose God's way instead of my way a remarkable sense of

peace enveloped me. I became content, no matter what the circumstances like the apostle Paul. I am able to sail through life's storms, troubles and trials, and stay on an even keel. Oh, I do get seasick from time to time when the storms are intense.

"I have learned, in whatever situation I find myself, to be self-sufficient. I know indeed how to live in humble circumstances; I know also how to live with abundance. In every circumstance and in all things, I have learned the secret of being well fed and of going hungry, of living in abundance and of being in need. I have the strength for everything through him who empowers me." (Philippians 4:11–13)

CHAPTER 5
Pool Water

"Water ... not necessary to life, but rather life itself; thou fillest
with a gratification that exceeds the delight of the senses."
—Saint-Exupery, Wind, Sand and Stars (1939)

The Secret: "Do not conform yourselves to this age but be transformed by the renewal of your mind, that you may discern what is the will of God, what is good and pleasing and perfect." (Romans 12:2)

Reverend Billy Graham once said, "When wealth is lost, nothing is lost. When health is lost, something is lost. When character and integrity are lost, all is lost."

Bill Crowder, Former Pastor, now author wrote, "The historic Riverwalk area of Savannah, Georgia, is paved with mismatched cobblestones. Residents say that centuries ago the stones provided ballast for ships as they crossed the Atlantic Ocean. When cargo was loaded in Georgia, the ballast stones were no longer needed, so they were used to pave the streets near the docks. Those stones had accomplished their primary job—stabilizing the ship through dangerous waters. The days in which we live can feel as turbulent as the high seas. Like sailing ships of old, we need stability to help us navigate our way through the storms of life. David faced danger as well, and he celebrated the character of God for providing him with stability after he had endured a desperate time." Remember to take on ballast.

The Lesson: "He lifted me out of the slimy pit; out of the mud and mire, he set my feet on a rock and gave me a firm place to stand." (Psalm 40:2)

David's experience was one of conflict, personal failure, and family strife, yet God gave him a place to stand. So, David sang "a hymn of praise to our God" (v. 3).

In times of difficulty, we too can look to our powerful God for the stability only He brings. His faithful care inspires us to say with David, "Many, Lord my God, are the wonders you have done, the things you planned for us" (v. 5).

My hope is built on nothing less than Jesus's blood
and righteousness; I dare not trust the sweetest frame,
but wholly lean on Jesus name. On Christ, the solid
rock, I stand—all other ground is sinking sand.
—Edward Mote

When the world around us is crumbling, Christ is the
solid Rock on which we stand. Psalm 40 is a beautiful song of
thanksgiving to God for His deliverance. The key to understanding
and appreciating this psalm is seen in the simplicity of the opening
words. David knows and celebrates the deliverance of the Lord
because he "waited patiently" for Him (v. 1). In our times of trial
and struggle, we want to be delivered quickly and in ways that are
simple to see. But David reminds us that God's deliverance comes
in God's timing. We, like David, must wait patiently for the Lord
if we are to see His wonders (v. 5).

> **The Lesson:** "For I know well the plans I have in
> mind for you—oracle of the LORD—plans for your
> welfare and not for woe, to give you a future of
> hope. When you call me, and come and pray to me,
> I will listen to you. When you look for me, you will
> find me. Yes, when you seek me with all your heart,
> I will let you find me." (Jeremiah 29:11–14)

God began the process of humbling me by first stripping away
all my wealth. I relied on our four children for financial support,
too proud to claim unemployment insurance. I struggled for two
years to find work after quitting my job instead of joining in a
fraudulent scheme.

Paula and I drove our twelve-year-old, 1984 Chevy Blazer, no
longer driving a big, expensive, shiny, new Cadillac. But we both
still had our health, character, and integrity, a roof over our heads,
and food to eat. We thanked God for these blessings. We lived God's

Way instead of My Way and committed to pursue His purpose instead of the world's pleasures.

> **The Lesson:** During eighteen months in the Pink House, I came to learn when God disciplines us our greatest gain isn't what we get but what we become. I am grateful for His grace and eager for His guidance.

Yet pursuing His purpose for me meant I had to find it first. Apparently, all of my prior positions and successes had not aligned with what He wanted me to do. Or perhaps they did, but I did not cooperate. Why else would He have me wandering the wilderness like the Israelites did for forty years? Feelings of being lost, no permanent home, loss of identity, jobless and without income?

While at the Pink House I practiced reading my Bible daily and attended daily mass with Paula. I had many questions but no answers. For eighteen months, I contemplated patience and destiny, patience and destiny, patience and destiny. I stood at these crossroads figuratively and literally, with the Pink House being located near the intersection of the roads to Lake Patience and Lake Destiny. I knew that God had brought me here for a very special reason other than to show me His sense of humor. He wanted me to do something with my life. But what? Like Moses and the people of Israel when they ran out of water in the desert, this place became my Massa (the place of the test). There I began personal prayer.

> **Personal Prayer Explained:** François Fénelon (1651–1715) wrote these words that explain personal prayer: "Tell God all that is in your heart, as one unloads one's heart, its pleasures and its pains, to a dear friend. Tell Him your troubles, that He may comfort you; tell Him your joys, that He may sober them; tell Him your longings, that He

may purify them." He continued, "Talk to Him of your temptations, that He may shield you from them: show Him the wounds of your heart, that He may heal them ... If you thus pour out all your weaknesses, needs, troubles, there will be no lack of what to say."

The Secret: "Don't be fools, then, but try to find out what the Lord wants you to do." (Ephesians 5:17)

The answer did not come instantly. It would take me several years to fully understand and appreciate my purpose. It took discipline, listening, humility, reading, contemplating, and abiding for me to come to the simple answer.

The Lesson: "Each day do something to inspire, to lift another soul out of the sea of sin, or disease or doubt into which mankind has fallen." (A. J. Russell, *God Calling*)

During my time in the Pink House, I secured interviews with three large corporations to become their president—and after pitching my accomplishments to each of the three board of director chairs, they rejected me one by one and chose someone else. Looking back, I suspect they recognized I no longer had the deep hunger for the road to more money, power, and prestige. My heart's desire strongly was now someplace else. Like the game of baseball, I had struck out after three pitches in a row. Frustrated, I told Paula maybe I should apply to be a Walmart greeter.

It was during this time I began the next step in prayer—meditation and contemplation. Sometimes the words seem to be interchangeable, but the practices differ. Sister Mary Colombiere of the Carmelite Sisters of the Most Sacred Heart of Los Angeles explains, "Let us begin by saying that the basic difference between meditation and contemplation is that meditation is a human mode of prayer whereas contemplation is divinely infused prayer."

In her autobiography, St. Teresa of Avila uses water as an image of various stages of prayer. Meditation corresponds to the first water. It is an invitation to contemplative prayer and is the characteristic prayer for all who are in this early stage of spiritual growth. Although meditation uses images, concepts, and reasoning, those means which are of the created order to commune with God, it includes nevertheless all forms of prayer in which human effort is quite active. The appetite is awakened to experience God's presence and gives us direction for our lives. When faith enlightens the mind, worldly things begin to lose their hold on us. We are drawn away from the "sensual" as we strive to unite our will with the will of God, and we express this through the virtue of our actions.

Contemplation is often a misunderstood word. It is not a prayer that we can initiate or cause to happen. It is divinely produced and no amount of action on our part can produce or prolong it. To return to St. Teresa's image of water, this is the second water, in which we still use a bucket, but the labor is less intensified since the water comes through an aqueduct and the use of a water wheel. The action here belongs to the Holy Spirit, and the work we do is only to dispose ourselves to receive the graces God is giving us. We have entered into a wordless prayer, an awareness of the divine guest within, not through the use of the intellect but through a knowing loving, a deep communion with the triune God. It is a prayer of quiet calmness in which we drink deeply at the life-giving fount. There are different intensities within this prayer, but the way of experiencing and the passion of the experiences will vary among individuals. Our external senses remain free and enable us to carry out our responsibilities and duties even when the interior faculties are captivated by God.

Contemplative prayer, therefore, does not belong to a privileged few. It is a normal common experience of the Christian life open to all. It is God's to give when and where He wills. Our preparation is to live the Gospel life and to be receptive to the graces God continually gives us—to be watchful and receptive.

One morning, soon after taking my morning walk in the orange grove, impatiently I shouted aloud with my fist raised to the heavens, "Lord, how long must I wait in this Pink House?" Thirsty, I then went inside for a drink of water, poured a cup of coffee, picked up my Bible, sat down and read this:

The Secret: "I am thirsty." (John 19:28)

The Lesson: Thirsty! I was overwhelmed. At that moment God spoke to my heart. "How long must I wait for you? I am thirsty." A chill ran up my spine! A profound realization, a turning point in my transformation.

In the months, ahead I sought more interviews, but none came. I continued walking in the grove, watching the orange blossoms slowly bud and the fruit ripen. I searched for my purpose and reflected on a remark by Mother Teresa, "We are not called to be successful. We are called to be faithful."

I realized that, with considered patience, what one decides about Christ determines the road to our ultimate destiny. I was at the crossroads of patience and destiny. Which would I take? Should I go down the road most traveled to money, power and prestige? I had tried three times to go down it, and each time I was blocked and turned around. Back at the crossroads, I waited, telling myself to be patient.

God, I said, "I believe you have a plan for me and a few more pieces to your puzzle need to put in place. I'll do things Your way. I will say yes. I will no longer say, 'No, I'll do it my way.' I will wait for you, perhaps others are not cooperating delaying your plan.

The most important words in a relationship are "Yes. I will. I'll do it." The next critical thing is to keep your words and do it. This develops your character. Are you a person of principles?)

The Lesson: "Just say 'Yes' or 'No.'" (Matthew 5:37)

I read the Bible cover-to-cover three times in the next few months. The words became clearer and clearer. It was like reading a novel. I couldn't wait to get to Revelations.

Several times a day I returned to the Pink House from my walks in the orange grove with an increasing desire, a hunger, to read the Bible, first as a book on the "history of mankind, second as a "how-to book on living," and third as a book of "personal conversations with God."

> **The Secret:** "Know this, my dear brothers: everyone should be quick to hear, slow to speak, slow to wrath." (James 1:19)

> **The Lesson:** The Listening Prayer—I have learned to speak less and listen more. Listening was, and still is, a struggle for me. I have learned though that when others speak to consciously be aware, to pause, and to hear what they are saying. Ego and pride are constantly lurking in the shadows, waiting for an opening to creep back in, but they can be suppressed and overcome through conscience self-discipline. The Holy Spirit can be heard through contemplation.

I have heard of meditation and contemplation and sometimes the words seem to be interchangeable. Is there a difference between the two? Let us begin by saying that the basic difference between meditation and contemplation is that meditation is a human mode of prayer whereas contemplation is divinely infused prayer.
—Sister Mary Colombiere, Carmelite Sisters of
the Most Sacred Heart of Los Angeles

Abiding with God daily prepared me to receive another spiritual gift called *discernment*. This gift must be developed. Discernment takes insight and awareness of the smallest details surrounding us. We must listen closely to what God is telling us.

> **The Secret**: "Let us be silent that we may hear the whisper of God."—Ralph Waldo Emerson)

We must search for clarity within ourselves for discernment. When we are in alignment with God's will, it will be clear, simple, and straightforward. You will not be anxious. You will feel freedom and calm. We can discern if we ask Him for direction.

Ask, *what is your will for me? What will you have me do? Help me discern. Give me an open heart to know which opportunities you want me to be a part of and give me wisdom in knowing how to carry that out. Amen!*

Then carefully listen for God's answer. As in all relationships, we must allow the other to speak while we carefully listen to what they say. Quiet your thoughts and pay attention. God has much to say. His timeless answers are recorded for us in the Bible.

> **The Lesson:** "Your Father knows what you need before you ask him." (Matthew 6:8)

> God hears you and will guide you. Listen closely and He will give you one of four commands to follow: "No," "Wait," "Slow," or Go."

1) No

You will not get what you want. You will get what you need. How do you know? You will be unsure, unclear, and uncomfortable. Your course will be full of strife and obstacles, little or no progress can be made, and you are constantly pushed back.

Doors to progress are closed. You, your crew, and your ship, or some combination of these, may not have been properly trained and prepared for the main voyage and what lies ahead. You could be at a temporary port, may have reached a wrong port or be going in the wrong direction, check your compass—the Bible.

The Lord appeared to him and said: Do not go.
—Genesis 26:2

2) Wait

You may need more preparation, practice, and coaching. Give thanks and praise. How do you know? When you receive the no command or are unsure of the command, be patient. Wait until you are sure. Wait until you are calm and at peace, clear on the direction.

"Wait for the Lord, take courage;
be stouthearted, wait for the Lord!"
(Psalm 27:4)

God is putting in place other pieces of the puzzle while you wait. People, things, situations, all need to cooperate before you can move ahead. New ports of call are being prepared for your arrival. He is sending ahead supply ships with fresh crews and provisions. They are on the way and must make port ahead of you. So, while you wait, rest, thank, praise, abide with God, quietly listening to Him and your advisors give you wise counsel on where to chart the course to your next port of call.

"Dwell in the shelter of the Most High,
abide in the shade of the Almighty."
(Psalm 91:1)

Thoroughly prepare yourself, select and train your crew, properly outfit your ship for the next voyage. Let there be no hurry in your plans. Relax, knowing that you live not in time but in eternity. Wait, prepare, and train. Your future is being prepared for you. Live a balanced life: work, personal, family, community. Just as athletes train for the contest.

> "Do you not know that the runners in the stadium all run in the race, but only one wins the prize? Run to win. Every athlete exercises discipline in every way. They do it to win a perishable crown, but we an imperishable one. Thus, I do not run aimlessly; I do not fight as if I were shadowboxing. No, I drive my body and train it, for fear that, after having preached to others, I myself should be disqualified."
> (1 Corinthians 9:24–27)

How will you know? You will sense the time is nearing to take action when this first thought comes to you, guidance, an idea of how to solve a problem, the solution to an issue that has been holding you back. You can now begin to make plans to move out, chart a new course only when your values align with the proposed direction.

> "For you will surely have a future,
> and your hope will not be cut off."
> (Proverbs 23:18)

3) Slow

You will know the planned course is right when you receive this next command.

> "Know this, my dear brothers: everyone should be quick to hear, slow to speak, slow to wrath."
> (James 1:19–21)

How will you know? You will be calm and at peace. You will know the time to depart is at hand. You will sense God is present when this second thought comes, reassurance. You know the crew and ship are ready, but you must still wait for the tide to rise. A few more things need to come into place.

Measure the water's depth, and when your ship's keel clears the bottom, let go the dock ropes that tie you. When you do, you will sense a newfound freedom. Instruct the crew to lower the ship's oars and slowly row the ship away from harbor's dock to the open sea.

How will you know? As you leave the harbor and reach the open sea, a third thought will come, a strong conviction. You are positive, no doubts. You know this is what you are to do. Now raise and stow the oars, drop anchor, and allow the ship to lie in wait just offshore. Rest, think about the results of the test trials, and listen closely for the next command. You may need to slightly adjust or modify your plan. Wait again for the tide to rise.

4) Go

You remain amazingly calm and not troubled, confident, sure of your direction, charts in hand, double-checking all preparations and your compass—the Bible. You may be anxious to act, but patience: you must wait for the next command. Patience, the command will come when all is ready, everything is in place, and the time is right. God is the great organizer. He created and operates the universe and everything in it.

How will you know? You will sense your soul being lifted like the feelings you get when you first smell the air of the open sea and fresh soft breezes beckon the sails. Inwardly you will know you have the peace of God, and it is now time to instruct the crew, "Take your posts. Prepare to sail! Hoist anchor! Then when the tide is up, doors are opened, and decisions become easy and obvious. You will know God's anointing you to go.

You watch as the wind picks up and steadily blows. You sense supernatural power (grace) flowing through you. It is during the listening prayer that we draw upon the power of the infinite God. When you feel this power you will know, "God answered: I will be with you ... Now, go! I am sending you" (Exodus 3:10,12).

It is time! Set the sails! Steady the wheel! Follow the course the Lord has laid before you. He will lead you.

We can't change the direction of the wind, but we can adjust our sails to reach the destination. "For those who are led by the Spirit of God are children of God" (Romans 8:14).

As the sails are hoisted they begin to fill with the wind then billow full and your heart does the same. The crew breaks out in loud cheers, shouts of freedoms joy as you get underway.

It is then that the fourth thought comes. You know God is present. You feel joy!

> "You will show me the path to life,
> abounding joy in your presence."
> (Psalm 16:11)

Sailing, you remain at peace, knowing that the fleet commander will guide you night and day through storms and heavy seas, so hold true to course through known and unknown waters.

> "Because you have kept my message of endurance, I will
> keep you safe in the time of trial that is going to come to
> the whole world to test the inhabitants of the earth."
> (Revelation 3:1)

Go! Full sail! Catch the wind. Explore. Dream. Discover. Enjoy. New adventures lie ahead. Smooth, safe waters are waiting for your arrival at the next port-of-call.

> "Go, therefore, and make disciples of all nations, baptizing
> them in the name of the Father, and of the Son, and of the holy
> Spirit, teaching them to observe all that I have commanded you.
> And behold, I am with you always, until the end of the age."
> (Matthew 28:19–20)

It is time! Set the sails! Steady the wheel! Follow the
course the Lord has laid before you. He will lead you.
We can't change the direction of the wind,
but we can adjust our sails to reach the destination.

"For those who are led by the Spirit of God are children of God."
(Romans 8:14)

I feel the winds of God today
Today my sail I lift.
Though heavy, aft with drenching spray,
And torn with many a rift;
If hope but light the water's crest, and Christ
My bark will use, I'll seek the seas at
His behest, and brave another cruise.
—James Abrams (1863–1954)

"Will your anchor hold in the storm of life,
When the clouds unfold their wings of strife?
When the strong tides lift and the cables strain,
Will your anchor drift, or firm remain?
We have an anchor that keeps the soul
Steadfast and sure while billows roll,
Fastened to the Rock which cannot move,
Grounded firm and deep in the Savior's love.
—Priscilla Jane Owens (1829–1907)

July 1996

After eighteen months in the Pink House, we were presented a
business opportunity that required a move to Jacksonville, Florida.
I picked up the Bible and the devotional reading of the day was
profound. It was as though God was speaking directly to me.

The Secret: "Remember how for forty years, the Lord, your God has directed all your journeying." (Deuteronomy 8:2)

The Lesson: This struck me deeply. I paused and reflected back on my entire life and to my first job after college with Westinghouse in Pittsburgh. Within ten years, I was national sales manager. Then I made a series of career changes to continue my climb up the corporate ladder to general manager and executive vice president.

Paula and I had made over a dozen family moves, back and forth across the country, East Coast, Midwest, Southeast. I thought, "Forty years!" Just Like Moses and the Israelites, I had been wandering the world, lost in my own desert, looking for the Promised Land. I had been shipwrecked and recovering at a desert oasis at the Pink House in the orange grove.

My friend Lou called me to ask if I had found work yet. (I was best man at his wedding to Lynda.) I told him no, and he asked if I'd ever thought of getting into the pool business. At the time, Lou was the New York–area sales representative of a Florida swimming pool chemical company, Girvan, Inc. I said I had not, but I told him that I had always enjoyed swimming and being around water. Lou introduced us to the owner, Don Girvan. We drove up to Jacksonville, and after meeting with him, he suggested I meet someone who wished to sell his business. I told Don we had no money. He said, "Don't worry about the money. You need to meet him." He arranged for us to meet Al Jackson, owner of Al Jackson Pools, founded in 1956. Al was nearing eighty years old and seeking to sell. I told Al we had no money. He said the same thing, "Don't worry about the money. Look at what we do and see if you like it." After a few days we went back to the Pink House. We prayed and asked God for discernment. Was this *where* He wanted us to go and do?

We referred to our Bible for an answer, and the daily devotional directed us to this reading:

The Secret: "Therefore, keep the commandments of the Lord, your God, by walking in His ways and fearing him. … For the Lord, your God is bringing you into a good country … a land with … pools and streams of water … with springs and fountains welling up." (Deuteronomy 8:6-7)

The Lesson: "Then he brought me back to the entrance of the temple, and there! I saw water flowing out from under the threshold of the temple toward the east … It was a river I could not wade across. The water had risen so high; I would have to swim." (Ezekiel 47:1–5)

It was an electric moment: Jacksonville, water, the ocean, the Intracoastal, the St. Johns River, pools and streams and fountains welling. Wow! Yes! This is where we are to go and do.

Al invited us to come back and take another look. He asked Paula if she would agree to work in the office and asked me if I would handle sales and oversee the construction crews. We said we would, and after some diligence, we agreed to a price. Al said, "I'll take a personal note of payment with monthly installments over the next ten years. Go over to the nearby branch of Barnett Bank and ask for a loan on the assets. Whatever they give you sign over to me as the down payment." We got the loan, and when we sat down with Al's attorney to close the deal, the matter of loan interest on the note came up. Al asked me to call the bank and ask if we were to deposit the amount of sale in a savings account, what would be the percentage of interest earned on it. I called and Al said, "Good enough," and directed the attorney to write it in.

Paula and I thanked and praised God for bringing us to a safe harbor. We formed a corporation to acquire Al's business and named it *Portofino*. I am Italian, and it's an Italian word for "a fine, safe harbor"—Portofino Pools.

Our governance established a board of directors, and we asked three others to join us: God the Father, the Son, and the Holy Spirit. All decisions must be approved by the board.

We laid out our plans, calculated revenues and expenses. We met with consultants, accountants, attorneys, and family members. Most importantly, we referred all key decisions to our board of directors. We worked to sell the concept to raise capital. We leased office/warehouse space, purchased equipment, acquired accounts, and hired employees.

We had one employee, Willie. The three of us worked hard, long hours, eighty a week, pouring ourselves into the business, determined to succeed. And it has. We have been nominated several times as "one of the top 100 Florida growth companies to watch."

In keeping our character and integrity, as Rev. Graham once noted, we have been able to rebuild the wealth we lost. But we now view at as a blessing from God instead of a testimony to our success.

> Having found his purpose for me, I do it
> His Way instead of My Way.
> Teach me to listen, Oh God,
> To Your truth and Your Way.
> —A. J. Russell

CHΛPTER 6
Healing

A reflection on John 21.
Jesus looks on him and forgives him. Peter is willing to accept Jesus' doctrine of forgiveness, but suggests a limit of seven times.

He walks on the water in faith, but sinks in doubt. He refuses to let Jesus wash his feet, then wants his whole body cleansed. He swears at the Last Supper that he will never deny Jesus, and then denies three times, swearing to a servant maid that he has never known the man. He loyally resists the first attempt to arrest Jesus by cutting off Malchus' ear, but in the end, he runs away with the others. In the depth of his sorrow, Jesus looks on him and forgives him, and goes out and sheds bitter tears. The Risen Jesus told Peter to feed his lambs and his sheep.

From sinking in the water when he doubted Jesus to denying him after his arrest, St. Peter's failings epitomized those of all of us. He was only human, after all. We too are weak. Forgiveness is available to all. Healing comes after we forgive ourselves and others. When we look deep within ourselves we will find in the shadows of our humanity failings and hurts that were tucked away perhaps years ago. These subconsciously work to prevent true rest, peace, and joy. Begin by forgiving yourself of your failings, then identify those that have hurt and harmed you. Forgive them, seventy times seven.

> **The Secret:** "If you forgive others their transgressions, your heavenly Father will forgive you." (Matthew 6:14)

Before the Pink House, I had failed to meet God's standards. I had put myself first, my personal wants, my ego for years and years. I am truly sorry, forgive me Lord.

> **The Lesson:** "You shall not have other gods beside me." (Exodus 20:3)

By doing so I had become infected with the worldly disease called *comparison obsession*. Marvin Williams describes this well in a 2016 article published in the daily devotional, *Our Daily Bread*. It is a reflection on Matthew 20:1–16.

> "Don't I have the right to do what I want with my own money? Or are you envious because I am generous?" Matthew 20:15. Thomas J. DeLong, a professor at Harvard Business School, has noted a disturbing trend among his students and colleagues—a "comparison obsession." He writes: "More so than ever before ... business executives, Wall Street analysts, lawyers, doctors, and other professionals are obsessed with

comparing their own achievements against those of others ... This is bad for individuals and bad for companies. When you define success based on external rather than internal criteria, you diminish your satisfaction and commitment."

Comparison obsession isn't new. The scriptures warn us of the dangers of comparing ourselves to others. When we do so, we become proud and look down on them (Luke 18:9–14). Or we become jealous and want to be like them or have what they have (James 4:1). We fail to focus on what God has given us to do. Jesus intimated that comparison obsession comes from believing that God is unfair and that He doesn't have a right to be more generous to others than He is to us (Matt. 20:1–16).

By God's grace we can learn to overcome comparison obsession by focusing on the life God has given to us. As we take moments to thank God for everyday blessings, we change our thinking and begin to believe deep down that God is good.

I need a better focus, Lord. Help me to keep my eyes off others and instead on You and Your good heart for all of us. God expresses His goodness to His children in His own way. Jesus taught the parable of the workers in the vineyard (Matt. 20:1–16) to show His disciples the generous heart of God. God is not unjust. He has no favorites and treats every Christian generously and equally (vv. 13–15). Paul later taught this same truth: "There is no favoritism with [God]" (Eph. 6:9; Col. 3:25). This extends to believers and the way we view others (1 Tim. 5:21).

The Secret: "Forgive us as we forgive others." (The Lord's Prayer)

Although God is always ready and willing to forgive us, He requires two things of us as conditions of forgiveness: repentance and forgiveness of others. Depending on the circumstances, confession (reconciliation) and restitution may also be needed. In seeking forgiveness in the name of Jesus, I have become more willing to forgive, personally and professionally. It is amazing how your perspective on life, yourself, and others changes when you do.

Two years after we moved to Jacksonville, I received a court summons for a hearing elsewhere in Florida. Legal action had been filed by former employees against my previous partner for withholding their rightful earnings. I was called to testify as to my knowledge of this matter, which had been the very reason I resigned. I recall sitting in the hall corridor outside the courtroom doors, shaking hands with the employees. When my former partner came around the corner of the hallway with his attorneys, our eyes locked. Initially his gait was quick and his stature erect. As I stood, his walk slowed, he turned slightly pale, and he bent forward as he passed. We did not speak or nod recognition. He then entered the courtroom.

I started to follow, but I was instructed to wait outside in the hall until called. After less than an hour, the courtroom doors opened. I expected to be called in, but everyone came out. The employees were all smiling, talking to each other. They shook my hand again and thanked me for coming. They said they had won. Soon, my former partner came out and approached me directly. He asked how I was doing since last, we'd seen each other. I told him a short version of the Pink House story. He was stunned and shocked when I told him I was now cleaning swimming pools.

He went on to say that had been certain he would win the case that day as he drove to court. But the tipping point was when he saw me outside the courtroom on his way in. He seemed crushed and told me he was sorry for what he did. I accepted his apology in forgiveness. I never saw or talked with him again. A year or two later, I learned that his business had failed, and a while after that, he had passed away.

This sadness and memory remains with me to today like a stone in my shoe. It reminds me to remain honest and trustworthy; to always conduct my business affairs with clients, vendors and employees with respect, candor, honesty, integrity; to do the right things and do things right. This is the genesis of Portofino's Beliefs, Values, and our BluDiamond Standards of Service.

Forgiving and accepting forgiveness in His name allows us to be forthright with one another. These core values have enabled us to grow our business. We continue to service pools that have been enjoyed by several generations of families that were built by the original founder, Al Jackson, in the 1950s.

Forgiveness forms the foundation for salvation. We can only be saved by Jesus. Accepting his mercy, His forgiveness, provides personal peace, even amidst life's greatest storms. I know this to be true. I've been there and experienced it.

The Lesson: "Repent and be baptized, every one of you, in the name of Jesus Christ for the forgiveness of your sins; and you will receive the gift of the Holy Spirit." (Acts 2:38)

The Miracle

In the summer of 2006, our middle son Paul, who lives in New York City, came to visit us in Florida for few days. He came down with a heavy rash on the left side of his forehead, and I took him to the hospital emergency room. They diagnosed it as shingles, unusual to be on the head, and they advised Paul to see his doctor as soon as he returned to New York.

He called after he return to New York and saw his doctor. The doctor sent him to a specialist to do a hip bone marrow biopsy and aspiration. After the procedure, Paul called again and described it was painful and scary, fully awake, hearing something like a hammer strike and as a spike was driven into his hip.

In a few weeks, he was diagnosed with bone marrow cancer, multiple myeloma, in advanced stage three. He was told he might have six months or more to live. Devastated, we were told there was no cure.

Paula and I booked a flight to New York City. Departing the next morning, we packed our bags for the trip, got into bed, and set the alarm clock. At midnight, we were awakened by our friend Deacon Larry Geinosky, knocking on our front door. He brought us a handmade blanket with a pocket containing a rosary. He explained it was for Paul. Some members of San Juan del Rio Catholic Church, our parish, had created a prayer blanket ministry for the sick. The ministry's members made blankets and on Sundays, at the end of every Mass service, the entire congregation, with raised hands, would pray for God to send His comfort and healing to those receiving the blankets.

Paul, after we gave it to him and returned home, told us he felt a special comfort envelope him when he covered with the blanket. He said he sensed that angels were all around him providing the comfort.

> **The Secret:** "So then, as often as we have the chance, we should do good to everyone, and especially to those who belong to our family in the faith." (Galatians 6:10)

Paula and I prayed and consulted the Internet. Paul called friends, seeking the best medical experts all over the country. By January 2007, Paul had been referred to a world-renowned cancer research doctor heading a specialized study on Paul's form of disease. He showed us a graphic time chart on his computer screen. It indicated how rapidly the cancer was spreading throughout Paul's body. He then made a statement that stunned and took our breath away. He said,

"Paul should be dead by now!"

Paul went on experimental chemotherapy and steroids treatment for another year. Then the doctor recommended a stem cell transplant. Paul was now in remission, but the doctor said that the cancer would come back. The transplant might prevent or at least delay it, perhaps for seven to ten years.

We were told most cancers are not eliminated 100 percent. Usually, best hope is for 60 to 80 percent. This is what they call "in remission."

We consulted experts in the Catholic Church and attended seminars on stem cell research.

Several men from our church volunteered to go to NYC with me, offering themselves for the transplant. Paula and I were awed. The love and concern of our parish community were beautiful.

Paula and I asked God to spare Paul. We offered our lives in his place. Deacon Paul Testa from our church offered himself for the transplant.

Eventually, our research found that our church leaders approved Paul's stem-cell procedure. He would be placed in a pressurized room with a double-air-door-pressurized entry. He would become a *bubble boy*.

His own stem cells would be harvested in several samples. Some would be sent to research. Some would be placed in a hyper frozen storage vault, should Paul need them in the future.

Another set would be treated with experimental chemicals and put through a special filtering process to remove the microscopic "bad guys." These stem-cells would then be transplanted back into Paul's body.

While waiting for the day of the second transplant we were told Paul would have no immune system for a couple of days. Hence the special hospital room. The drama was incredible.

A few months earlier, Danny Brown, a member of our church whom I call my spiritual brother, invited me to go on a road trip with him and a few other guys. He had asked me a several times before over the course of a few years, about every six months or so. I said no every time.

Typically, when you go on a road trip with a bunch of guys you commonly stop at a few bars along the way. I really was not interested. Those days had been left far behind. I thanked again, but asked,

"Where are you going? This time" Golfing? Major sporting event? Fishing or Hunting?

Every time I asked in the past, Danny would never tell me the destination of these trips. He would just smile and say you "got to go to know".

This time he told me. We go on silent retreats to the Monastery of the Holy Spirit in Conyers, Georgia."

I said, "What?"

After further explanation of the details, I agreed to go with him and thanked him for the invitation.

The trip had a profound impact on me. God's timing was perfect!

The fellowship of my Christian friends, talking with the monks inside the monastery walls, the quiet times in the chapel, walks in the woods, it all let me see God in a new perspective—and to pray for Paul's healing.

Over the next few months Paul's weight plummeted to 130 pounds, and he seemed to age twenty-five years before our eyes. His hair turned gray and then some started falling out. He could sleep for an hour or two at a time.

The day of his procedure, Paula and I were there with him in New Your City. When they removed his stem cells, they blasted him head-to-toe with massive chemo to destroy all cancer cells in his body. His immune system was completely wiped out.

Soon Paul's white cell count dropped to zero. Paul had the worst skin sunburn and blisters we ever saw. Both on the outside of his body from his face and lips to inside his mouth through his entire digestive system. And many very unpleasant side effects as well. He lost another fifteen pounds. He was in agony.

Paul told me, "Dad, my insides are on fire, and all my bones feel like they want to burst." He rated the pain as a one hundred on a scale of one to ten.

As he told me this, an image of Jesus suffering the day He was crucified for our sins came into my mind. I thought this was how Jesus must have felt the day he in earned our forgiveness.

Before the procedure we were told it would take two, maybe three days at most, before they would do the second transplant. This while they processed the stem-cells and that Paul's immune system needed to re-start.

Paula and I were permitted to stay with him in his special room, but we had to follow strict rules of sanitizing on entry and could not touch him. We waited and prayed. And prayed.

Deacon Bob Gardner, one of our Christ Renews His Parish Ministry team members, told us how he had felt the pain of his brother while he suffered from cancer. Bob said, you share the pains of someone you love.

In the middle of all this, our financial pressures escalated. We had lived very frugally since the Pink House, but the cost of traveling and living in NYC combined with being away from our business quickly drained our resources. Additional medical treatment costs, Paul's insurance would pay the majority of the cost but—the transplant procedure alone was more than $500,000—. When submitted Paul's insurance company refused to pay and he asked me to call and debate them. The bills piled and pressure built. Finally, Paul was told the hospital would waive any bills the insurance company refused to pay. Thank you the hospital and thank you God!

It was now approaching day seven since the first procedure, Paul's immune system was not regenerating. He was weakening fast, suffering, slipping away. The doctors said his body was shutting down. I kept telling Paul, "You must fight!"

Later in that evening, I was reading my Bible while sitting next to Paul's bed. He awoke and looked over at me as he clutched the medal around his neck of the Archangel Michael. He whispered, to me, "Dad, I don't have the strength to fight anymore." He just stared at me with a deep longing look in his eyes. Time was running out. It was supposed to be but 2, at most, 3 days. It was now the end of day seven.

I left the room to find the doctor. When I did I told him, "you must do something and do it now!"

He said, "We have exhausted all that science can do. Paul may not make it. We expect the immune system to regenerate within 2 to 3 days at most. After that chances of survival decline rapidly. It is now seven days, prepare yourselves.

His immune system needs the *mystical spark of life*, like a jump start of a car battery. We don't know how to do that."

I told Paula and we went downstairs to the ground floor hospital chapel and prayed in earnest,

"Dear God, modern science has done all it can do. I praise you. I worship you. I thank you for everything. May Your will be done... Please, Lord, ...I ask for a God incident. Please create that spark of life in Paul."

We left the chapel. Paula went back to Paul's room. I telephoned everyone I knew, including the Monastery of the Holy Spirit. I explained the situation to the person that answered and to please

Ask the monks to pray right now for the Spark of Life for Paul Manilla.

I called the people of my church. They sent a broadcast e-mail out to our church prayer chain. I told everyone that I could:

"Paul needs a jumpstart from God!
Pray right now for the Spark of Life for Paul Manilla.

I went back up to Paul's room. I told Paula I had called everyone and asked for prayers right now. We held each other's hands as we watched Paul's breaths get slower and slower. We each asked God to take us instead of Paul. We had lived full lives. Allow Paul to so.

We waited in the silence.

A monitor connected to Paul started beeping. A nurse came in checked the instrument and drew a blood sample from Paul and left the room. She kept returning every 5 to 10 minutes checking the monitor. Paula and I feared the worst.

The nurse returned and told us the results of the blood sample confirmed the monitor.

"We've found a white cell count, and it is rising rapidly!"

Stunned, we asked the nurse, "What happened?"

The nurse replied, "A miracle. Paul got the spark of life. Your prayers did it."

"Look at the graph on the monitor screen! It is tracking Paul's immune system.

It is going straight up!"

Soon dozens of hospital staff were coming in the room with us and glad handing each other. We hugged the senior doctor and he confirmed,

"A miracle. Paul got the spark of life! Prayer did it."

The Secret: "But now we must celebrate and rejoice, because your brother was dead and has come to life again; he was lost and has been found." (Luke 15:32)

One week later, on Dec. 1, 2007, Paul was released from the hospital and sent home.

We were shocked. They had told us that Paul would be in the hospital for six weeks after the transplant, he was only in the hospital fifteen days before his blood count was back to normal. The cancer was gone—100 percent.

By April 2008 he was working full time. He remains well and is still with us to this day.

CHAPTER 7
Gratitude

There once was a young boy with a very bad temper. The boy's father wanted to teach him a lesson, so he gave him a bag of nails and told him that every time he lost his temper he must hammer a nail into their wooden fence.

On the first day of this lesson, the little boy had driven 37 nails into the fence. He was really mad!

Over the course of the next few weeks, the little boy began to control his temper, so the number of nails that were hammered into the fence dramatically decreased.

It wasn't long before the little boy discovered it was easier to hold his temper than to drive those nails into the fence.

Then, the day finally came when the little boy didn't lose his temper even once, and he became so proud of himself, he couldn't wait to tell his father. Pleased, his father suggested that he now pull out one nail for each day that he could hold his temper.

Several weeks went by and the day finally came when the young boy told his father that all the nails were gone.

Very gently, the father took his son by the hand and led him to the fence.

"You have done very well, my son," he smiled, "but look at the holes in the fence. The fence will never be the same."

The little boy listened carefully as his father continued to speak. "When you say things in anger, they leave permanent scars just like these. And no matter how many times you say you're sorry, the wounds will still be there. —Author unknown

> **The Secret:** Be grateful for all that you have been
> given and all that you can do.

> "Instead, be filled with the Spirit, speaking to one another with psalms, hymns, and songs from the Spirit. Sing and make music from your heart to the Lord, always giving thanks to God the Father for everything, in the name of our Lord Jesus Christ."
> (Ephesians 5:19–20)

Each morning, I wake up and I thank, praise God and tell Him I am sorry for saying things that hurt other people the day before ... knowingly or unknowingly. I ask Him to guide me and make me into the better person He wants me to become this day before me.

I tithe the first hours of the day to be with the Lord, before the sun comes up. This is when I am fresh and full of energy. Oh, it's all right if you pray in the evening, but I don't like to give God my prayer leftovers at the end of the day when I am tired and may forget. For me, it's

"No Bible, No breakfast."

The Lesson: Give thanks and praise. "It is good to give thanks to the LORD, to sing praise to your name, Most High, to proclaim your love at daybreak, your faithfulness in the night" (Psalm 92:1–414).

As I get of bed in the morning, I thank God by praying:

"God the Father, Son and Holy Spirit, I love you! It's me, Jack.
Thank you for loving and protecting Paula and me through the night.
I praise you and give you thanks for all the
blessings you have given us. Amen!"

Flawed though I may be, I thank Him for making me who I am. Some say I am stubborn, others strong willed. I err often and sometimes my emotions erupt over innocent remarks. My dad taught me to be a competitor and a fighter. I used to strike a word punch back at offending remarks by others. I now, most of the time, smile and ignore or say kind words.

I prayerfully thank God throughout the day for having a plan for my life and helping me to live it—through the good times and bad.

It has taken me a lifetime to learn to trust in God and to discover this most valuable truth: I am not in charge of my life, nor anyone else's for that matter. I have come to trust that life unfolds just as it should. We must trust the Holy Spirit and get our controlling selves out of the way.

Lose your ego. Create an attitude of gratitude. Focus on "How may I serve you?" Not "What's in it for me?" Strive to be gracious and kind versus being right.

Start each day focused on how we may thank God. Say by helping others as He has helped us, by applying the gifts He has provided. By "paying it forward" by helping others improve their lives.

Portofino Pool Services & Outdoor Living provides weekly and monthly in-house training sessions for its employees. This to help develop them professionally and personally. Our company is known for its unique *BluDiamond Standards*, developed to build character, strong values, which ensure customers that each employee is trustworthy, knowledgeable, skilled, and experienced in servicing their needs.

I have channeled dual passions for helping others and for raising the bar of professionalism in my industry...*Portofino University*. Founded in Jacksonville, Florida 2005.

Portofino University has become an international provider of certification courses and training for commercial and residential aquatic facility managers, technicians, contractors, and owners. In honing their knowledge, students can use the education we provide to advance their careers and enhance their standards of living.

Portofino University has let me work with and assist thousands of professionals whom I may not have otherwise met. It has established me as a thought leader in the industry. I am grateful for having these opportunities to serve others.

I spent five weeks at sea, consulting for Royal Caribbean Cruise Lines, training their Western Pacific Fleet ship officers and crews on how to maintain safe and enjoyable pools. I hadn't solicited the company's business. Rather, others sought me. I would the favor of visiting fourteen ports of calls in seven foreign countries of the Far East including New Zealand and Australia.

In 2014, I was asked to do a round of training in Trinidad and Tobago, West Indies. I helped establish pool health and safety standards for the country. I had also helped Trinidad professionals become professional certified pool operators by teaching a sixteen-hour CPO® course. Which provides essential knowledge of how to reduce risks in and around the water, including understanding and preventing recreational water illness, suction entrapment, diving accidents, chemical hazards, slips and falls. They were also trained in the process of disinfection, water balance, water problems and corrections, chemical testing, record keeping, and chemical feed systems. Such topics were largely new to the Trinidad pool operators at the time.

They had no government codes and no voluntary industry standards. There were no guidelines, standards or regulations like we have in the United States. As the guest speaker at an evening reception, I shared two books on industry standards, published by the Association of Pool & Spa Professionals (APSP). I explained the difference between mandatory government regulations and voluntary industry standards and best practices and encouraged them to pursue the later through a rigorous process that results in consensus.

They had told me that they would voluntarily pursue best practices as professionals who wanted to provide the best health and safety for their residents and tourists.

Establishing standards in Trinidad and Tobago like those in other countries would positively impact public health and safety for their whole country. Opening their eyes and enlightening them on safe, healthy pool operations was highly rewarding. Paula accompanied mon this trip to Trinidad and greatly assisted me in class. We were grateful for the opportunity to help so many by sharing our business experiences.

"Praise the LORD, for he is good; for his mercy endures forever;
Praise the God of gods; for his mercy endures forever; Praise
the Lord of lords; for his mercy endures forever; The Lord
remembered us in our low estate, for his mercy endures
forever; Freed us from our foes, for his mercy endures forever;
And gives bread to all flesh, for his mercy endures forever.
Praise the God of heaven, for his mercy endures forever."
(Psalm 136:1–3, 23–26)

CHAPTER 8
Humility

"Remember that you have been sent for the salvation of
people, not because of your own merits, since it is the Lord
Jesus and not you who died for the salvation of souls."
—St. Leopold Mandic

I stopped living large when I arrived at the Pink House. But I
didn't start living right until I left. The eighteen months in between

humbled me, forcing me to accept that the life that was gone was never coming back.

Luxury cars. Pool homes. Private jets. I had once defined myself by what I had. But I had come to see that all that really mattered was who I was and the love that Paula and I shared.

Paula led me to this realization. I cannot count how many times she had told me that the earthly possessions that I had so prized were "just things." She often reminded me that those weren't important to her. She was content with us having our health and each other. I came to understand and feel likewise.

I always remember we were ready to move into a double-wide trailer home if that was to be our new life. I also was ready to become a greeter at Walmart after striking out in my attempts to restore myself to my former glory. Before we left the Pink House, I had interviewed for three senior management positions at Fortune 500 companies, but none had materialized. Gradually, with Paula's help, I came to believe that the Lord would see us through whatever was to come.

The day I got the call to go into the pool business after eighteen months in the Pink House, I had to accept that it was God's Will and I was to start my career completely over.

"Now go, I will assist you in speaking and teach
you what you are to say." (Exodus 4:12)

We were, and remain humbled to this day, very thankful for our children who stood by and helped us: our daughter Jackie and son John sent money monthly, our son Brad provided us free rent and utilities for The Pink House, our son Paul paid the down payment on Portofino and paid our Jacksonville apartment rent for 2 ½ years. He also paid the down payment on our new house and carried the mortgage in his name until the bank would approve a new mortgage in our names. Paul then sold it to us for $1.00. For several years we had to ask him for approval of any business expenditure over fifty dollars during the initial years we owned and operated the business, as he was now a partner in Portofino. The first year we owned Portofino our total gross revenue was $50,000 before we paid any business expenses: retail store, office and warehouse rent, parts, equipment, chemicals and subcontractor fees, licenses permits, business insurance, part-time help wages, government taxes...the list went on and on.

As the father who had once splurged on the children to whom God had entrusted me to provide, each humbling circumstance was another test of how far I was willing to go to be meek. I had once thought of meek as weak, but have come to see it very differently. My life is in the Lord's hands. I now do my best to listen to what God wants of me and go do it.

> **The Secret**: Remember the Lord your God, for it is he who gives you the ability to produce wealth." (Deuteronomy 8:18)

> **The Lesson:** Obedience, "Blessed are those who hear the word of God and obey it." (Luke 11:28)

Humility has brought success. Portofino has prospered by serving and doing work that others would not. Pool maintenance and cleaning had long been looked down upon by peers in the industry because it lacks the pride and glamor of new construction. But the willingness to submit myself to His will and do what others weren't doing helped me develop a successful business model because pool owners, especially commercial accounts like hotels, resorts, private schools, and condominiums were indeed willing to pay for high quality services

Though we spent the first two years of Portofino building pools and operating a retail store, our very first job was, in fact, a pool pump motor repair. The former owner had recently completed a renovation and the pool owner called to say that the pump making loud noises. So, I grabbed a tool bag and went to see what the problem was. I replaced the motor with a new one and the customer was very happy with our promptness and paid me right then. That was my signal that I should emphasize repair and equipment replacement services.

Next this customer asked me to clean and maintain their newly remodeled pool. They had invested thousands of dollars in improving it and wanted to ensure the equipment was being serviced properly and the pool would be taken care of in a professional manner. Another signal to offer maintenance services which would be invoiced every month. I wouldn't need to keep looking for someone who wanted to have a pool built.

When we did decide to focus on maintenance after barely surviving for two years doing new construction, many pool builders told me, *"You don't want to be a pool cleaner."* But I had put my ego in check by now.

Sufficiently humble, I went door to door, block after block and solicited pool services. I picked up 35 contracts to clean pools each week and did the work myself. As word spread, more people started calling our office and asking Paula for pool services. So, we could afford to hire a technician to do the route. I hired one and trained him on how to test, analyze and treat the pool water to drinking water standards. I spent the next five years as the head pool cleaner building service routes, and hiring and training technicians until we had several hundred customers. Then one day told me, *"I would like my old Jack back without dirt under his fingernails every night when he comes home from work. Next Monday come to the office and be the service manager."* I returned to the office and continued to focus on growing the business.

I reached back to my childhood memories and corporate career to refine the business model that fueled Portofino's service growth—that is providing customers with peace of mind, allowing them to enjoy their pools by providing them excellent service.

My father had run a railroad-construction business part-time.

The bulk of his work was repairing and maintaining private railroad spurs from the main line into manufacturing plants. I observed that while everyone else was chasing new railroad construction he could do as much work, if not more, in profitable maintenance jobs.

Also, when I worked at Westinghouse after graduating from college, we would spend up to two years helping architects and engineers design vertical transportation (elevator and escalator systems) for high-rise office buildings, only to have to bid for the actual equipment and construction against many others who had not invested the free engineering consulting. Competition was so fierce at best, if we won the job, we would break even. The pay-off came when you were awarded a service contract agreement to maintain the equipment for the life of the building. So, maintaining, repairing, replacing and remodeling elevator equipment became the moneymaker for Westinghouse—not new construction. I duplicated this business model.

> "You have to get to a place where you scare
> yourself before you can better yourself."
> (Martin Luther)

In addition to recognizing the business opportunity that was available to us because nobody was focusing on services in the pool industry, I had the willingness to pursue it because I was humble in my commitment to serving others.

When people told me that I didn't want to be servicing pools, I told them I was meant to be of service to others. That is one of the reasons that Portofino has thrived. Being genuinely meek and humble has helped us help our customers relax and enjoy, to de-stress when coming home from a hard day's work by jumping in their pool or just hanging out by it with a cool drink.

The commitment to serving others permeates our entire staff, allowing us to pick each other up and help each other out. Nobody puts themselves above others. Paula will scrub the toilets at the office and regularly scrubs carpet spills. I'll pick up staples and paper clips from the floor and take out the trash.

We don't wait for someone else to do something that we could do ourselves, no matter how menial or trivial it may seem. If we can't clean and care for where we work, we can't tell others that we can do likewise for their home or business.

I have long been part servant and part business person but until I had hit rock bottom in the Pink House I had put myself first. Only in hitting rock bottom, and learning from Paula's unfaltering love and devotion, did I learn true humility and meekness. Only in setting down my ego by submitting, did I rise and Portofino thrive.

> **The Secret:** The law of 10-fold. What you put out is what you get back, 10 times more.
>
> If your intentions are positive and good, from a God praising, humble, thankful heart, and you put out: positive thoughts, emotions, energy, (I.E. service to others), what you will get back will be multiplied ten times.
>
> **The Lesson:** "Make no mistake: God is not mocked, for a person will reap only what he sows. Let us not grow tired of doing good, for in due time we shall reap our harvest, if we do not give up." (Galatians 6: 7-9)

Love, praise and give "thanks always and for everything in the name of our Lord Jesus Christ to God the Father and the Holy Spirit" (Ephesians 5:20).

CHAPTER 9
Love

"You shall love the Lord, your God, with all your heart,
with all your soul, and with all your mind. This is the
greatest and the first commandment. The second is
like it: You shall love your neighbor as yourself."
(Matthew 22:37–39)

The ancient Greeks recognized different types of love. And
while love does take many forms, its power is constant. Whether it

is our devotion to a spouse or our caring for a sick loved one, when we love, we put others before ourselves and will do anything on their behalf.

I've been blessed with abundant love. From the parents who doted on me and siblings who nurtured me, to the wife who has loved me unwaveringly and the children and friends who have loved and supported us endlessly, I am grateful to God for all of the love that I have received. I also am thankful for the love that I have given because that is what we are called to do. Most importantly I have been most fulfilled when I have loved and helped others in times of their need.

> **The Secret:** The way we came to know love was that he laid down his life for us; so, we ought to lay down our lives for our brothers. If someone who has worldly means sees a brother in need and refuses him compassion, how can the love of God remain in him? Children, let us love not in word or speech but indeed and truth." (1 John 3:16–18)

I have learned the love of God through the amazing gifts that He has granted, including the calling to share my story, *The Secrets of the Pink House, From Saltwater to Holy Water*, so that others may find personal peace by abiding in his love and grace. I have learned how to love unconditionally, Paula the perfect model. She has never stopped loving me, regardless of circumstance. She has believed in me even when I have not believed in myself.

Men tend to shape their self-identity according to their work and accomplishments. When I had nothing to point to, as a breadwinner without bread, Paula found reasons to rejoice, like the fact that we had others to love and be loved by others.

> **The Lesson:** "We must consider how to rouse one another to love and good works." (Hebrews 10:24)

I have also learned love through friendships. If you show respect and kindness to others, it comes back to you tenfold. I once dropped everything to accompany a friend for a few days on a thousand-mile trip one-way. A trip he did and didn't want to make. We had become close friends and he had shared his concerns about his sister who had been seriously ill for a long time. When she passed away, he wanted to go home for her funeral, but there was lots of conflict and turmoil within the family from the past, and some people he just didn't want to see. Without hesitating, I offered to go with him. We flew out the following day. We ended up staying with some of his close family and all went well. Expected confrontations did not occur.

Though this was indicative of the love of giving, another instance may be one of the greatest examples of the powerful love of an enduring friendship I was blessed to have experienced—my friendship with A Johnson. I met Al through Christ Renews His Parish, a ministry process at our church, but we bonded through hardships. First, Al was there for me, and then I was there for him.

When we were moving our business into a new office, I dislocated my right arm when I fell while carrying a fifty-pound pail of pool chemicals. It was one of the worst pains that I felt in my entire life. I couldn't move my right arm. The next morning, I went to an emergency room. They took x-rays and the doctor reset it, putting it back into the socket, by pulling my arm out of the joint while pushing his foot into my ribs. He said the pain would subside soon after, but it persisted. I went to my family doctor and requested an MRI he said to wait longer. The pain will subside. My arm hung listless at my side and I was unable to move it in any direction.

After three months, of asking I finally convinced the doctor I should have the MRI. Magnetic resonance imaging (**MRI**) is a test that uses a magnetic field and pulses of radio wave energy to make pictures of organs and structures inside the body. Within 24 hours the doctor called me to come to his office right away. He said the main muscle tendon in my shoulder socket, the one that enables arm movement in all directions had been completely severed when my arm had pulled out the socket. And when it snapped back at an angle the bones completely cut, severed, it. I would need surgery to repair the ligament and I would have find a surgeon to do it. I was recommended to a skilled orthopedic surgeon and he agreed to do it, but I would need to wait another three months to get a date on his schedule. He was in high demand. The pain continued.

Knowing that I couldn't drive a car for three months, Al volunteered to be my chauffeur. He was out of work at that time. So, helping me made sense to him. Every day for the next three months, he came to my house helped me put my shirt on for work, drove me to job sites, and then took me home at the end of the day. That's a friend's love. We had great conversations and Al was angry about many things. I did my best to counsel him. We were drawn ever closer.

The surgery was difficult and took many hours. The doctor shared that he made several attempts to extend the tendon like a rubber band. In the six months since the accident It had shriveled back to my neck. The surgeon was concerned that it would break off as he pulled it. He placed several stainless-steel posts into my collar bone and as he extended the tendon he tied it off to each post. By the time he reached the last post the tendon was extremely thin and kept snapping back. After several failed attempts, he paused and said he prayed to God, *"Lord if this is your will, please give me the skills and strength to complete this procedure and extend this tendon's stretch to the piece of tendon attached to the arm where I can tie them together. Thank you! Amen!"*

He resumed the work gave the tendon one more pull and it was successful tied. I would need another six months of rehabilitation physical therapy, and Al continued to drive me around, to work, to rehabilitation several times a week, and then back home. Al was my personal driver for a year. That was a friend's love.

A year or so later Al asked me to drive back to his old hometown in far North Dakota, along the Canadian border to bring back to Florida a classic pickup truck he had stored in a barn for years that he wanted to restore. I quickly agreed to go with him. We drove up and back, total round trip 4,000 miles, completed in forty-eight hours. Now that was *road* trip. I was thrilled that I could make this run with him, and we had a great time visiting along the way.

A few years later, Al was divorced. He was very distraught when he called to tell me that he was going back to North Dakota to live for good. Worried that he shouldn't drive such a long distance by himself when he was upset, I volunteered to make the trip with him. This was my turn to love Al. We stopped overnight at motels a few times on this journey at my insistence. I was able to meet several of Al's family and friends and flew back home to Florida.

We stayed in touch by phone and several years later Al was diagnosed with pancreatic cancer and given just a few months to live, I flew up to visit with him. He was staying with his brother north of Minneapolis, MN. I asked Al if he would like to go to church the next day. When we got up on Sunday morning it was forty degrees below zero. We ventured out but couldn't find a Catholic church open due to the cold. Rather than going to another denomination, Al asked me to drive to the cathedral in downtown Minneapolis. He said it was always open, and when we got there it was.

Al was a singer in the navy's top choral group while he attended the United States Naval Academy in Annapolis. We sat in the very front pew and Al sang out sweetly but quite loudly in praise and worship during the Mass. He drew many smiling glances. He grinned from ear to ear, pure joy across his face. One would not know he was dying.

Al lived for two more years, going in and out of hospitals for much of that time. Finally, accepting that he wouldn't live any longer he sold all his belongings and used the funds to fulfill his bucket list. One of his dreams for years was to sail the Caribbean Sea. So, he chartered a sixty-foot catamaran sailboat replete with a captain and a chef. Al invited me to join him for week sailing to nowhere out of Key West, Florida. Al flew from Minneapolis and I flew from Jacksonville. Coincidentally (a God Co-Incident) we ended up on the same connecting flight from Tampa to Key West—in the same row, sitting right next to each other. Talk about a "God-incidence."

After spending a night at a luxurious hotel (my gift to Al) and visiting with other friends who drove down from Jacksonville, Al took all of us on a chartered deep-sea fishing excursion. The next day Al's daughter and a friend of hers from college, joined us and we set sail on out into the Caribbean Sea. Al, the captain, and I shared sleeping rooms in one of the yacht's hulls, while the women occupied rooms in the other hull.

I helped Al keep up with his medications taken every few hours around the clock. Al carried an extra suitcase just for the medications. We spent a week sailing under sunlight blue skies, and evening stars. Stopping wherever and whenever we wanted. We would drop anchor, go for a swim, snorkel and launch a small rubber boat, taking it to explore many uninhabited islands. It was a wonderful trip—and the last time I would see Al alive. We continued to talk by phone almost daily until the very end.

When Al passed away, his ex-wife (also a friend of a Paula and I) called to tell me and that the funeral would be in Minnesota. Their family hadn't been churchgoers for many years and she asked if I could do the funeral service myself or get someone to do so. Deacon Larry Geinosky from our church is a good friend and knew Al. He asked me if he could hold the service. We flew together to Minneapolis, Minnesota.

Al's family appreciated us coming. We brought love to the family and got many hugs and wet cheeks in return. They were grateful that we flew from Florida to handle the services and show our love. Al's ex-wife asked us to organize another service for Al at our church in Florida, so those who knew Al could attend. This was held awhile later. To me, it was only natural to do so. Al had done so much for me when I was in need that I wanted to pay his love forward.

Whether our love is for a friend, spouse, family member, or stranger, it binds us together and provides us power—the power to love and beloved. That is what we are called to do.

"Love never fails. If there are prophecies, they will be brought to nothing; if tongues, they will cease; if knowledge, it will be brought to nothing. For we know partially and we prophesy partially, but when the perfect comes, the partial will pass away. When I was a child, I used to talk as a child, think as a child, reason as a child; when I became a man, I put aside childish things. At present we see indistinctly, as in a mirror, but then face to face. At present, I know partially; then I shall know fully, as I am fully known. So, faith, hope, love remain, these three, but the greatest of these is love." (1 Corinthians 13: 8–13)

CHAPTER 10
Maturity

"It is not that I have already taken hold of it or have
already attained perfect maturity, but I continue my
pursuit in hope that I may possess it, since I have indeed
been taken possession of by Christ [Jesus]...Forget what
lies behind but strain forward to what lies ahead...
continue pursuit toward the goal, the prize of
God's upward calling, in Christ Jesus...
For our citizenship is in heaven."
—Philippians 3:12–14

Spiritual maturity is defined by Reverend Ed and Cheryl Henderson, in their book *Ultimate Success … God's Way*:

> "There are three stages to spiritual growth.
>
> *Childhood* is the first. Until a little one learns to walk there is a lot of tripping and falling. Realizing and understanding there is a difference between this stage and the next, standing, is critical to growth. Trusting and believing fully in Jesus Christ gives right standing with God. From this point on every time you fall Satan will make you doubt. But remember forgiveness is always available as you are now a member of God's family in good standing.
>
> *Adolescence* is the second stage. The transition from teenager to adult can be tumultuous. Finding one's way, questioning everything, trying different things, rejecting discipline are all part of this stage. The truth is the spiritual adolescent thinks they know it all and really doesn't. They need guidance, support, encouragement and plenty of direction. A good spiritual director, mentor, is very important during the stage.
>
> *Adult* is the third stage. Knowing God. (Not just knowing *about* God). How do you know when this occurs? When you comfortably abide with the Lord, like you do in a close friendship or marriage. Just hanging out together provides love, respect, happiness; and joy. It is the result of spending time with the Lord daily. It is a lifetime commitment. It is the same as exercising the body to get and stay in shape."

"There are good ships and wood ships, ships that sail the sea, but the best ships are friendships, may they always be!"
— Irish Proverb

The Secret: "But as it is written: What eye has not seen, and ear has not heard, and what has not entered the human heart, what God has prepared for those who love him, this God has revealed to us through the Spirit." (1 Corinthian 2:9)

The Lesson: The spiritually mature see things the average person does not and hears things sharp ears do not. Thoughts come that one does not originate because the Holy Spirit is helping us to think God's thoughts. This doesn't just happen. It takes daily work. It's not an afterthought or a once week Sunday morning thing. It must become your top life-long passion. What stage are you in? *Childhood, Adolescence, or Adult*

Discernment: Samuel said, "Speak, for your servant is listening" (1 Samuel 3:10).

You will know you are a spiritually mature adult when God allows you to grasp new thoughts and insights from reading His words in the Bible. These thoughts go far beyond what you may have heard others say before. This will occur when the Holy Spirit flows freely through you, the pipe, the channel. You will be free of controlling human thoughts and doubts, the debris that blocks and restricts, thus allowing the "living water" of knowledge and understanding to flow freely. "So that we may understand the things freely given us by God" (1 Corinthian 2:12).

"God has communicated in various ways throughout history (Hebrews. 1:1). One-way God speaks today is through our conscience (Romans. 2:14–16). Our conscience is like a moral monitor. An important way we discern whether a spiritual

129

communication has God as its source is to ask: Does the message agree with the Bible, God's written Word? If it does not align with God's previously revealed truth, then we cannot put our stamp of approval on it." (Amy Boucher Pye)

Since the days in the Pink House, our journey has been one of slow but continuous transformation, a journey to spiritual maturity, an ever-increasing depth of knowledge and understanding. I learned through faith, endurance, and suffering to place my trust fully in God. I consult with Him daily on all decisions, business, family, and personal.

As a result, I have found new hope and a more fulfilling life. Oh, I still am stubborn, and I struggle with my stubborn will. At times, I catch myself rushing ahead and making decisions on my own without first consulting God, Paula, and my wise counselors. On the occasions, I act alone (unless they are like past situations and issues where I previously consulted others for direction), I find that I am wrong when rushing to snap decisions. Now when I err, I try to learn from my mistakes.

My goal is to keep maturing spiritually and to balance that with physical and intellectual maturity. I strive to balance work, family and community—to be the same person regardless of circumstance. I constantly seek knowledge, understanding and discernment. I work on the discipline to apply that knowledge in mature judgements . We all walk a similar walk up the spiritual ramp to maturity.

The Secret: "Teach me wisdom and knowledge, for in your commandments I trust." (Psalm 119:66)

Before the Pink House, I had thought of maturity only in terms of chronological age, physical maturity and eventually intellectual maturity. But I had never considered my spiritual maturity until I was forced to do so.

In examining my relationship with God, I found many opportunities for spiritual growth. I had a passion for knowledge. Reading the Bible repeatedly was the start. I consumed books on all sorts of spiritual matters as well. I have read dozens of books on the mystic saints of the church who lived in the middle ages. I strove to acquire spiritual knowledge wherever possible. I had always hungered for knowledge, but now it was channeled for spiritual know-how instead of worldly skills.

Long before the *Pink House*, Paula and I had lived in the *Brown House* when we first married. We would sit on the front-porch swing of this single-bedroom lake cottage, planning our future. Things we wanted do, places we wanted to see, people we would like to meet. I told Paula that I never wanted to be sitting in a rocking chair when I was old saying,

I could have … I would have …
I should have … I was always going to.
I coulda, woulda, shoulda…I was gonna…

If ever I had an opportunity for something new, I would consciously decide whether to do something or not, I would seek as much knowledge and understanding, and consider possible outcomes of doing it. This process continues today for me in my spiritual journey.

The Lesson: Fear of the Lord is the beginning of knowledge; fools despise wisdom and discipline. (Proverbs 1:7)

One of noted benchmark that confirmed I was maturing spiritually was my pastor's appointment to the leadership role of the Christ Renews His Parish ministry. My name was submitted at the request of the founding leader in our parish, Deacon Jerry Turkowski.

I had tutored under his direction for several years in a variety of roles within this ministry. For 15 years I participated in leadership roles or oversaw 45 weekend retreat teams, comprised of 12-24 men and 12-24 women each. Each team would study, discuss and train in weekly meetings for six months in advance of presenting a Men's or Women's Retreat Weekend twice a year, in the Fall and in the Spring.

During these weekends, the teams would present 12 individual, twenty-minute talks, sharing their life stories. We would tell how we fell-down, then got-up, perhaps only to fall again. And in sharing our weaknesses we became strong.

Live. Fail. Learn. Repeat. The more I saw the pattern in my life and those of other men and women in the program, the better able I was to convey the never-ending nature of our quests for maturity.

> **The Secret:** "Consider it all joy, my brothers, when you encounter various trials." (James 1:2)

Listening to the stories of hundreds of men over fifteen years, reflecting and relating the events in their lives to my own accelerated my maturity. I was inspired by the many real life transformations I witnessed, and confirmed by their subsequent willingness to volunteer to help others experience a weekend and by their sharing their personal stories at future retreats.

> **The Lesson:** We are all in a trial now, coming out of trial, or heading toward the next one. Don't try to get out the way prematurely. Let it do its work so you become mature, as James says, "So that you may be perfect and complete, lacking in nothing" (James I:4).

> You will never get bored because trials come in "various" ways you can never imagine.

The opening words of James 1:4 are, "And let *perseverance* be perfect, so that you may be perfect and complete, lacking in nothing." Perseverance is key to your advancing, moving forward in maturity. I will discuss this further in the next chapter.

Still, not knowing my own level of maturity, my leadership was openly tested. I disagreed with how a weekend team leader, Danny Brown, was preparing to run his upcoming weekend retreat. We locked heads in disagreement over issues on how the process of the weekend should be run, and I took my concerns to Deacon Jerry for advice.

I closely followed the handbook of policies and procedures. Danny was a creative thinker and loved to improvise. Deacon Jerry knew Danny personally for many years. He confirmed he walked to a different drumbeat, but always with the best of good intentions and achieved excellent results.

Deacon Jerry decided to speak with him to see if he could get his friend to conform. He told him to stick to the program's strict agenda instead of departing and creating new steps. I attended this weekend as I also was this team's spiritual co-director. I was determined I would ensure that Danny did as he was told to do, but of course he did not. He veered from the agenda. I was angry. I told him so. He just couldn't comprehend my position.

Danny called me a few months after that weekend. He invited me to go with him on a road trip that he was taking with a few other men. He said he wanted us to make-up our friendship after our dispute and the trip would provide the perfect means to so.

At first, I rebuffed him, saying that I knew too well from experience that a "road trip" was nothing more than a mislabeled hunting or fishing trip that provided cover for lots of carousing at bars along the way. He insisted that wouldn't be the case but never would tell me the destination. After much consideration, I agreed to go, even though on the morning he picked me up he still wouldn't tell me where we were going.

The road trip that I had first refused to take would become one of the best experiences in my entire life. God has a plan for each of us. We just need to cooperate.

Upon arriving at our destination, after a six-hour car drive, I was totally surprised to find that we were driving into the long driveway entrance of the Monastery of the Holy Spirit in Conyers, Georgia.

My vision at Safety Harbor had taken place at the Church of the Holy Spirit, and now I was at a monastery coincidentally named "the Monastery of the Holy Spirit." I couldn't help but think this was yet another God-incidence. I had a wonderful, insightful experience, soaking up new knowledge imparted by the monks in their seminars, so much so that I have continued to make it a habit of an annual road trip to the monastery with a few close friends. We continue the tradition of inviting new men to go with us on a " road trip", keeping them in suspense as long as we can, so we can enjoy their surprise. All have been very thankful for the experience.

My first Christ Renews His Parish weekend retreat triggered massive spiritual growth in me. I realized then that we never stop maturing spiritually. We're always either stopped, going forward, or going backward down the spiral ramp. If when we pass on and are fortunate enough to be invited into heaven, I am certain maturing will continue forever. God is infinite and has so much to teach us that we will need all eternity to learn.

Though our perception of "maturity" here on Earth may be limited, we must constantly push ourselves. As I said, I have returned to the monastery often, including married couples retreats and large church-group visits. I learn something new every time.

Though I have matured spiritually, compared to where I was years ago, in the Pink House, I never stop thirsting for knowledge, for new growth. Nor should of any us, because God wants us to grow, know and love Him more, year by year, day by day, moment by moment.

Where on the Spiritual Ramp will you be
when your earthen journey ends?

The Secret: "Make every effort to supplement your faith with virtue, virtue with knowledge, knowledge with self-control, self-control with endurance, endurance with devotion, devotion with mutual affection, mutual affection with love. If these are yours and increase in abundance, they will keep you from being idle or unfruitful in the knowledge of our Lord Jesus Christ. Anyone who lacks them is blind and shortsighted, forgetful of the cleansing of his past sins." (2 Peter 1: 6–9)

"We squander health in search of wealth. We scheme and toil and save, then squander wealth in search of health and all we get is a grave. We live and boast of what we own, we die and only get a stone."
—Author unknown

The Lesson: "Train yourself in (spiritual) devotion, for, while physical training is of limited value, (spiritual) devotion is valuable in every respect, since it holds a promise of life both for the present and for the future." (1 Timothy 4:8)

"It is not that I have already taken hold of it or have already attained perfect maturity, but I continue my pursuit in hope that I may possess it, since I have indeed been taken possession of by Christ [Jesus]. Brothers, I for my part do not consider myself to have taken possession. Just one thing: forgetting what lies behind but straining forward to what lies ahead, I continue my pursuit toward the goal, the prize of God's upward calling, in Christ Jesus. Let us, then, who are "perfectly mature" adopt this attitude. And if you have a different attitude, this too God will reveal to you. Only, with regard to what we have attained, continue on the same course." (Philippians 3:12–16)

"But I will call upon God, and the Lord will save me. At dusk, dawn, and noon I will grieve and complain, and my prayer will be heard."
(Psalm 55:17)

CHAPTER II

Perseverance

"Keep on doing what you have learned and
received and heard and seen in me.
Then the God of peace will be with you."
(Philippians 4:9)

Paula and I recall the bliss of young love. At nineteen years of age, we were the world, and the world was perfect here we were. Then reality hit—children, my career, life's surprises.

Our perfect world became a world of ceaseless challenges. Each seemed harder than the last. Life tried to pull us apart and in many directions. Each storm tested our devotion to one another and to our marriage. But our love was and is true…we persevered—and focused on our faith in God to pull us through. In doing so, our young love became mature love, capable of seeing us through many storms and a tsunami.

We have helped other couples persevere as well. As counselors for engaged couples, we talked about how to keep little nothings from becoming big fights, like preventing a squabble over who left the cap off the toothpaste tube from escalating into a major fight.

We learned to communicate and share our feelings. Though I tend to be quiet at home, Paula can sense if something is amiss and we will tackle the challenge together. A good rule is to kiss and make-up before getting in bed for the night. A few times we stayed most the night.

> **The Secret:** "See, I refined you, but not like silver; I tested you in the furnace of affliction for my sake, for my own sake, I do this; why should my name be profaned? My glory I will not give to another. Listen to me, Jacob, Israel, whom I called! I, it is I who am the first, and I am the last." (Isaiah 48:10–12)

> **The Lesson:** God wants to use our difficulties to strengthen our faith. God leads us. We just need to follow and move forward.

Demons may try to overcome us. Like on a battlefield we must continuously advance or be overrun. If some falls, pick them up and carry them, If the flag bearer goes down, pick up the flag and press on valiantly toward the goal. Say what the US Marines say, "HUA," (Hoo-aaah) it means "Heard, understood, and acknowledged." I have kept moving forward since the Pink House, hearing, understanding and acknowledging God's guidance, day by day, hour by hour, and moment by moment. HUA! Just as we are to

SECRETS OF THE PINK HOUSE

follow the Lord's commands, we should also follow our spouse's requests and do so willingly. When Paula asks me to do something, most of the time I say, *"Yes. I'm happy to."* But I often fail in taking the next step by saying, *"I will do it now."* And then take the last step, *"Go and do it!"*. Don't put it off, saying, "I'll do it later."

> **The Secret:** "Teach me wisdom and knowledge, for in your commandments I trust." (Psalm 119:66)

> **The Lesson:** Perseverance is one of the secrets to a good marriage as well as a secret to a good relationship with the Lord.

Perseverance is doing something—even when you don't really want to—and doing it willingly, with a smile on your face. Humbly accept it and move forward.

Perseverance is also about making the most of our challenges, like losing our health or loved ones. My dad was one of thirteen children, and I grew up with many aunts and uncles. I had more than one-hundred cousins, most of whom gathered at Grandma Mary Manilla's house every Sunday afternoon for meals and kid's games, while the adults sat around and visited.

Time winnowed the ranks of my immediate family and relatives, eventually leaving just my older sister, Arlene and me. I visited my sister, who lives in Ohio, during the early fall of 2016, she remarked how it was just her, me, and a few cousins left.

My visit reminded me of my sister's inner strength. She is only two years older, but medical problems have sapped much of her physically, making me fit by comparison, but she has remained vibrant as ever.

My sister Arlene Joan Manilla Egelsky hasn't walked in several years. She is 90 percent paralyzed from the waist down and has had 95 percent hearing loss since birth. Confined to a bed in the living room of her daughter's home, her legs fill with water before eventually escaping her body through painful blisters. Once or twice a year Arlene is hospitalized as the sores become infected, and they must give her special medical treatments.

My niece, Wendy Darlington, her primary caretaker, along with Wendy's two sons, Jake and Zack, must get her out of bed with a manual lift so that they can change the bedsheets.

When I visited, my niece, Wendy cranked up the lift, transferring my sister from her bed to the La-Z-Boy in the living room, which had become her bedroom. My niece did this several times during my visit, which lasted from a Friday to the following Tuesday. I was struck by how she so lovingly cared for her mother. She had probably never thought she would have to do so when she was growing up. Yet Wendy persevered. Her two sons, Jake and Zack, would also take turns lifting my sister out of bed and bringing her meals.

A few years after graduating high school Zach moved out and was working a steady job in one of the mills. He and his fiancé, Elizabeth, had a baby boy they named Jaxson. Arlene and Jaxson have a joyous time together when he comes to visit several times each week.

Wendy shared a car with Jake. He would drop her off at work at 7:30 a.m. each morning before going to college classes and then to his part-time job, before picking up his mother and bringing her back home, where she would prepare dinner for the family and again care for my sister without complaint. Wendy worked a full-time day job and for many years then left for a second night job. She persevered even though she herself suffered with multiple sclerosis for years. Every six months Wendy would travel to the Ohio Cleveland Clinic for treatments.

It would have been easy for any family in such circumstances to gripe about how life was unfair and to turn upon one another bitterly. But my sister, my niece, and her sons celebrated life instead. During my visit, we had a great time watching the Jacksonville Jaguars football game on TV on Sunday afternoon. Arlene surprised me by putting the game on TV. Both boys, Elizabeth, and Jaxson all gathered with us in the living room. We ordered takeout food and tailgated, all of us munching on snacks through the afternoon, cheering, shouting, and talking about good times from our pasts. The Jaguars won that game. (It was one of only two wins and twelve losses for the 2016 season.)

I returned to Jacksonville knowing that my sister would now be getting seven-day visiting nursing care at home. She was also getting in-home physical therapy, three times a week. Arlene told me she was determined she was going to walk again, even if it was just a few steps to move around the house. Forward! An example of perseverance personified!

I was happy knowing that she was being so well cared for by my niece and that their perseverance would soon pay off in the form of more help.

Unfortunately, a few months after my visit, my niece passed away unexpectedly. While I was visiting, Wendy had told me she was having migraine headaches and that her mind was going crazy. We all shook this off because Wendy had always been a uniquely funny character. She had gone to the local hospital twice before my arrival, and after several hours, they sent her home each time with pain medicines that they attributed to her M.S.

A month later, the condition worsening, she traveled to the Cleveland Clinic for diagnostic tests. They changed her MS meds and sent her home as well. On the drive, back home with Elizabeth driving, Wendy blacked out and was hallucinating. She could not recall where she was. Liz drove her straight to the nearest hospital.

Wendy went into a coma for the next two weeks. After the first week a close family friend and nurse, Lisa, strongly encouraged they do a spinal tap. She was diagnosed with severe meningitis. Neither Lisa or Wendy had no siblings and were like sisters growing up together, having lived right next door to each other until graduating high school. Lisa was now a neurological nurse living in Pittsburgh, but she traveled to be with Wendy.

Arlene requested to be transported to the hospital when they were about to remove Wendy from life-support systems. After a few days, they moved Wendy to hospice where she quickly passed away.

Paula and I flew to Pittsburgh, rented a car, and drove to see Arlene and family in Ohio and attend the funeral service. We then flew on to Michigan for the Thanksgiving holiday with our oldest son's family. Arlene had a difficult time coping with Wendy's passing. She would be taken to hospital ten times in the next eight months, then diagnosed with cancer, she passed away peacefully on July 22, 2017 with me and my two nephews by her side.

"Blessed are those who mourn for they will be comforted."
(Matthew 5:4)

> **The Secret:** "Therefore, since we have been justified by faith, we have peace with God through our Lord Jesus Christ, through whom we have gained access [by faith] to this grace in which we stand, and we boast in hope of the glory of God. Not only that, but we even boast of our afflictions, knowing that affliction produces endurance, and endurance, proven character, and proven character, hope, and hope does not disappoint because the love of God has been poured out into our hearts through the holy Spirit that has been given to us."
> (Romans 5:1–5)

> **The Lesson:** Persevere. Though life had struck us another blow, a surprise attack to me and my sister as well as our family of loved ones, we move forward—just as God wants us to do.

CHAPTER 12
Service

Jesus summoned them and said, "You know that the rulers
of the Gentiles lord it over them, and the great ones make
their authority over them felt but it shall not be so among
you. Rather, whoever wishes to be great among you shall be
your servant; whoever wishes to be first among you shall be
your slave. Just so, the Son of Man did not come to be served
but to serve and to give his life as a ransom for many."
(Matthew 20:25–28)

Growing up on *Service Avenue* in Sharon, Pennsylvania, I can't
help but think of "service" very often. Helping others becomes
ingrained in you when you grow up seeing your parents doing for
others all the time.

My father easily could have spent his whole life working for himself and his family, but he didn't. The second oldest of thirteen children, he went to work for the Erie Railroad at the age of sixteen, right after his father died unexpectedly. My dad, Vito, became our family's patriarch and grew strong as a provider for us, lugging around steel rails for the railroad and for his own business, which he ran part-time on the weekends in addition to working full-time for the railroad during the week.

With arms bigger than my thighs, he also made money as a practice squad player for two professional football teams, the Pittsburgh Steelers and Cleveland Browns. They often would ask my dad to bring with him the biggest guys working in the steel mills for practice scrimmages in return for a few dollars each and lunch.

An avid sports fan who would simultaneously watch a game on TV while listening to one on the radio and reading the sports page, my father saw the practice squads as a way to help the teams while helping his family. He was so good at it that when the Pittsburgh Steelers won their first Super Bowl in the 1970s, they took him to the White House with them to meet the President of the United States. My dad was invited to bring my mother as a guest with him. But my mother was sick, and rather than anger my brother, myself, or my sister by selecting one of us over the other, he told know one about where he was going for a few days. Dad went by himself and only told us afterward. He just did not want jealously or strife to enter the family. They sent a limousine to carry him to the 75 miles to the Pittsburgh airport where he boarded a private charter aircraft with the Steeler players, coaches and owners. After cake and ice cream and meeting the President, they flew back to Pittsburgh and the limousine drove my dad back to our home in Sharon. My dad taught me much in life by his actions.

> **The Lesson:** And what you heard from me
> through many witnesses entrust to faithful people
> who will have the ability to teach others as well.
> (2 Timothy 2:2)

I learned the value of service from my father by following his political career. Somehow, between family, football and work he found time to serve on the city council, eventually being elected its president.

My mother also served our community, as a charter member of an association for businesswomen in the 1950s. She had returned to work when I was old enough to tend for myself and gradually worked her way up the corporate ladder, becoming a buyer for a major department store, traveling twice a year to New York City and Chicago on spring and fall buying trips. I would drive the family car to the store where she worked and drive her home everyday.

Paula's parents similarly served their community, the smallest government incorporated village in Ohio. Her grandfather had founded it, and when he passes away, Paula's father was elected to serve as the village's mayor for decades, from the time turned twenty-one years old to when he died. Paula's brother was then elected mayor and contuse to serve this day. Her mother served as village clerk, and when we both lived there, Paula was elected to the village council and an older brother was sheriff.

Whenever someone had a problem, they went to Paula's family for help. Once, a small circus came to town, and its performers were poor and needed food. Her dad bought them all groceries, and the circus manager gave him a giant, stuffed bear as a thank-you gift. That bear has since been handed down through the generations of Paula's family as a reminder and symbol of service to others. Paula's mom would often say she never knew how much money her father had given away to help people.

> **The Secret:** "The people rejoiced over these free-will offerings, for they had been contributed to the Lord wholeheartedly. " (1 Chronicles 29:9)

In addition to being community servants, my parents were

always steady churchgoers. They showed me how to live a balanced life, working multiple jobs, volunteering serving others and renewing their faith during Sunday services.

Paula and I moved so much during my career that we decided to build our social lives around the church wherever we lived. We have always been involved in our church, helping others and serving in many ministries—you have to reach out and be part of something greater than yourself.

Paula often reminds me of how many dear friends we have made through the church. So many wonderful people are in our lives that might not have been if we hadn't sought a way to serve.

Already running Portofino Pools full-time, I didn't have much "spare" time to commit to the association, but serving my industry is a way for me to give back or as they say pay it forward, so I welcomed the opportunity to help.

With my parents as my role models, I have always seen the value of combining work and service. I want to help others because of my life experiences. But since the Pink House, I have become more intent on being a person who serves God, family, and community. No longer do I strive for personal riches in private while preaching benevolence in public.

I have woven service to God and others into my work life and my personal life. I have become myself. I am Jack and I am content. I live a balanced life of marriage, family, work, church, community, and industry volunteer service (www.linkedin.com/in/jackmanilla).

Over the years, as we moved from city to city and state to state, I was drawn to join a variety of ecumenical religious groups, lay leaders with broad representation of spiritual beliefs who worked together to find and develop common beliefs to unite the local community and beyond. Currently, I am a member of a hybrid faith-based group of business owners here in Jacksonville called Wise Counsel. It was founded by John Beehner, who also is a former founder and operator of a Florida-statewide business round table of executives that he sold several years ago and is called Vistage. I have found the members of Wise Counsel to be extraordinarily deep in both spiritual and earthly wisdom, and they to service their churches and the community in many ways small, large and very large missions to the world. (www. askwisecounsel.com).

One member in my Wise Counsel round table group of advisors is Bryan Hickox, an award-winning writer, producer, executive producer, and director of feature films, long-form television, and series television programming (www.bryanhickox.com). Bryan introduced me to Bishop Robert (Gosselin), a global voice of unity (www.counttoone.com). Pope Francis has charged Bishop Robert with uniting Catholics, Protestants. and Charismatics for Christ.

I am often challenged and asked about my Catholic beliefs and practices and I answer to the best of my ability. Recently I read an article in the magazine *St. Augustine Catholic* November/ December issue 2016, written by Lilla Ross about Dr. Edward Sri of the St. Augustine Institute in Colorado. You might know Dr. Sri from EWTN or from one of his many books, including *Mary: A Biblical Journey from Nazareth to the Cross*. Dr. Sri articulates well my personal beliefs and practices and much better than I possibly could. He writes, "What makes a great Catholic? Following the rules? Yes, we need to follow the rules, but He's calling me and you to do more than that. He's calling me and you to enter into a relationship with Him. Are we Jesus disciples? Are we really striving to imitate the master, to grow in holiness?"

"I will honor those
who honor me"
(1 Samuel 2: 30)

November 10, 2015

Mandalay Bay Convention Center, Las Vegas, Nevada

The Association of Pool & Spa Professionals

Designates

Jack Manilla, CBP, CSP

APSP Fellow

In recognition of contributions and thought leadership
at the frontiers of the Pool & Spa industry, and for
exceptional potential to shape the future of the industry
through intellectual and inspired leadership.

Teaching – Research- Service

2015

September 30, 2016

It was a hot Florida evening as I took the main stage at Jacksonville's Oktoberfest 2016. This was the signature event of Portofino Pool Services & Outdoor Living's Sixtieth Business Anniversary celebration and the twenty-year milestone of our entering the pool industry and leaving the Pink House.

Many of our customers, vendors and friends, along with thousands of families were enjoying the annual celebration at the Jacksonville Budweiser Brewery. They were reveling in a variety of entertainment, including live music, dancing, and a smorgasbord of authentic German cuisine, traditional festival fare, and thirst-quenching beers. Mike White, president of CFM, our marketing agency, arranged for us to be a sponsor and for me to tap the keg with the Brewmaster to open the weekend ceremonies.

November 1, 2016

It was a clear, mild evening in New Orleans, Louisiana and the excitement of taking another stage after earlier that day being seated as chairman of the board of directors of the swimming pool industry's largest and oldest international trade association in the world had me feeling queasy inside. We were attending the Association of Pool & Spa Professionals Annual International Awards of Excellence during the annual International Pool, Spa and Patio Exposition.

I was a long way from our home in Jacksonville and I was glad Paula was with me as we entered Celebration Hall. I tried to convince myself this was not a dream. I went backstage as the presentations began, and while I waited my turn, I congratulated and shook the hand of each person being honored before they stepped out from the curtains.

When my name was called, I told myself, *"You will not faint or trip and stumble. Just go one step at a time."* I then walked onstage to be recognized.

Though my eyes were blinded by the bright lights, I felt Paula's warm smile and heard the audience's loud cheers and extended applause. They embraced me. I relaxed. I was home.

Humbled, I gave several bows and in my heart thanked the Lord for this honor. At that very moment, a memory surfaced from the museum of my mind. I was amazed how far God had brought Paula and me from those lost, questioning days in the Pink House twenty-one years ago. The excitement and wonder of this evening will never leave me.

About APSP

The Association of Pool & Spa Professionals (APSP) is the world's oldest and largest association representing swimming pool, hot tub, and spa manufacturers, distributors, manufacturers' agents, designers, builders, installers, suppliers, retailers, and service professionals. Dedicated to the growth and development of its members' businesses and to promoting the enjoyment and safety of pools and spas, APSP offers a range of services including professional development, advocacy at the federal and local levels, consumer outreach, and public safety awareness. APSP is the only industry organization recognized by the American National Standards Institute to develop and promote national standards for pools, hot tubs, and spas. For more information, visit **APSP.org**.

December 28, 2016

Several weeks later I was presented a surprise award in Jacksonville, Florida, by the Southside Business Men's Club. I had been named the *2016 Small Business Person of the Year*. The award stated, "In recognition of your leadership and achievements as a business owner and embodiment of the attributes and qualities most important to the Southside Business Men's Club since the awards inception in 1988, and commensurate with its namesake, Dyess Hartley."

I humbly thanked the presenters, the officers, board and members of the Southside Business Men's Club for selecting me for this honor. Their collective support and confidence in my leadership and achievements was very rewarding.

It has been quite the year to be recognized for service nationally and locally. It has been my privilege to serve alongside the more deserving members of these great organizations. Whether giving back or paying it forward, I am confident each organization's and Portofino's best days are ahead.

Some things in life are better experienced than explained. 2016 was a highlight year for us and I am humbly reminded of what my dad and mom would often say to me at such times.

"Well, it's a good beginning!"

The Lesson: "I trust in you, LORD; I say, 'You are my God.' My destiny is in your hands." (Psalm 31:15–16)

You and I share an important soul mission and life purpose that involves communicating, teaching and healing others and serving humanity in a manner that suits each of our unique talents best. I encourage you, the reader to serve, to Inspire others, to seek their own passion and purpose in life as you now do. Set a positive example for others.

"If you want to identify me, ask me not where I live, or what I like to eat, or how I comb my hair, but ask me what I am living for, in detail, ask me what I think is keeping me from living fully for the thing I want to live for—Christ!"
—Thomas Merton

That's a question we need to ask ourselves and each other—daily!

EPILOGUE

"Do not conform yourselves to this age but be transformed
by the renewal of your mind, that you may discern what is
the will of God, what is good and pleasing and perfect."
(Romans 12:2)

My past life was about what I had. Power. Prestige. Possessions. Privilege. I defined success much in the same manner as the western world defined success. I derived happiness through my belongings. I drew pride from my accomplishments.

Then God shipwrecked me on the rocks at Safety Harbor, Florida. I was then led to the Pink House in an orange grove and found the spring of holy water. I learned secrets and lessons that transformed my mind and my life.

Now, when life's inevitable difficulties come, I steer through the storms with personal peace and serenity by applying the Pink House Secrets and Lessons.

1. **Saltwater**—While at the Pink House, for months I was in a battle of positive over negative, good over evil. It was like I was on a beach with ocean waves washing in over the sands that ebb and flow, then a large one would come in, knock me over, and tumble my body into the surf of despair. Disoriented, I would again complain to God. It would take months to change me. I finally realized I had not truly changed. I kept trying to do it my way and not God's way.

I kept trying to go back to Egypt to rejoin my old life. My Way is not self-way. My Way is God's way.

2. **Holy Water**—Core values taught by the world conflict with those in the Bible. Scriptural virtues such as humility, kindness and respect for others versus hubris, for example; to live simply instead of seeking power, status, and prestige; generosity instead of hoarding; self-control instead of self-indulgence; and forgiveness instead of revenge. We strengthen and tone the soul through grace that comes with knowledge, understanding, and discernment of the Word of God. Keeping our spiritual heart strong and fit must be our first priority, the one thing we do above all others.

3. **Chameleon**—I worked hard to climb the corporate ladder, but I schmoozed my way up as well. I acted differently in public than I did in private. I did what I needed to do to get ahead, even if it wasn't always right to do. My actions were grounded in my personal hubris instead of divine principles. The Pink House taught me to be one person at all times, at work, at home, and in the community. I am no longer a chameleon who changes colors to suit their circumstances.

4. **Choices**—We want to do right, but we do wrong. Even if we have been spiritually transformed, we still make wrong choices as we are human, and our old nature always remains. Tempting thoughts of all sorts still creep into your mind. Remember to call for help when these battles come. When you are faith-led, you can make a life-changing choice for everlasting happiness in the great eternity instead of the easy choice that leads to a short-term life of temporal gain here on earth.

5. **Pool Water**—It took me several years to fully understand and appreciate my purpose. It took discipline, listening, humility, reading, contemplating, and abiding for me to

SECRETS OF THE PINK HOUSE

come to the simple answer that what one decides about Christ determines the road to our ultimate destiny. I learned to pray and ask God for discernment. In doing so, he led me to Jacksonville, Florida, where I would I use the opportunity that He provided to buy a pool company to restore my career and rebuild my life.

6. **Healing**—Although God is always ready and willing to forgive us, He requires two things of us as conditions of forgiveness: repentance and forgiveness of others. Depending on the circumstances, confession (reconciliation) and restitution may also be needed. In seeking forgiveness in the name of Jesus, I have become more willing to forgive, personally and professionally. I have witnessed God's remarkable power to heal as a result.

7. **Gratitude**—I thank God every day when I wake up. I praise Him and tell Him I am sorry for hurting other people. I ask Him to guide me and make me into the better person He wants me to become. I then tithe the first hours of the day to be with the Lord, just before the sun comes up. This is when I am fresh and full of energy. God gives you His best when you give Him your best and thank him for what he has already given to you.

8. **Humility**—I stopped living large before I arrived at the Pink House. But I didn't start living right until I left there. I had long been part servant and part businessperson, but until I had hit rock bottom in the Pink House, I had put myself first. Only in hitting rock bottom and learning from Paula's unfaltering love and devotion did I learn true humility and meekness. Only in setting aside my ego by submitting did I rise and Portofino thrive.

9. **Love**—When we love, we put others before ourselves and will do anything on their behalves. I learned the love of God through the gifts that He has granted, including the calling to share my story so that others may find personal

peace by abiding in His love and grace. I also have learned how to love unconditionally through Paula. Love binds us. We are called to love.

10. **Maturity**—Since the days in the Pink House, my journey has been one of continuous transformation, a journey to spiritual maturity, an ever-increasing depth of knowledge and understanding. I learned through faith, endurance, and suffering to place my trust fully in God. I consult with Him daily on all decisions, business, family, and personal. As a result, I have found hope and a new, richer life.

11. **Perseverance**—God leads us. We follow by stepping forward in faith. Perseverance keeps us pushing ahead through life's storms. We overcome the storms and find personal peace by always keeping our eyes on Jesus and striving ever forward to meet Him.

12. **Service**—We are called to help others. It may seem as if you don't have time to do so, but you do. The secret is to embed service into your life. It isn't something you schedule. It is something that you do. In helping others, you will help yourself, knowing that you are fulfilling one of God's primary purposes for your life.

If you had asked me to tell my life's story when I was strolling the orange grove at the Pink House, I would have told you it was all about me. I would have said that I had attained all that I had ever aspired to and I would have blamed God for taking it from me—even though I had done what was right.

Now, looking back, I can say that the darkest times in my life were merely the dawning of the brightest days that were to come—and that I have God to thank for delivering me to the personal peace that followed the storm.

—Jack Manilla

Excerpt from Pilate's Letter to Tiberius Caesar concerning Arrest, Trial, and Crucifixion of Jesus

(Note: Gives physical description of Jesus)

From the *Archko Volume*, containing manuscripts in Constantinople and the records of the Senatorial docket taken from the library at Rome, translated by Drs. Macintosh and Twyman of the Antiquerian Lodge, Genoa, Italy.

This has been checked and is in accord with the copy of the original lodged in a British Museum that has verified the accuracy of the transcription. The original, longer letter, was more than five thousand words long. It was verified in November 1935.

To Tiberius Caesar, Emperor of Rome

"When the great excitement arose about the sepulcher being found empty, I felt a deeper solicitude than ever. I sent for Malcus, who told me he had placed his lieutenant, Ben Isham, with one hundred soldiers, around the sepulcher. He told me that Isham and the soldiers were very much alarmed at what had occurred there that morning.

I asked him [Isham] if he had been questioned by the priests. He said he had. They wanted him to say it was an earthquake, and that they were asleep, and offered him money to say that the disciples came and stole Jesus, but he saw no disciples; he did not know that the body was gone until he was told. I asked him what was the private opinion of those priests he had conversed with. He said that some of them thought that Jesus was no man; that he was not a human being; that he was not the son of Mary; that he was not the same that was said to be born of the Virgin in Bethlehem; that the same person had been on earth before with Abraham and Lot, and at many times and places.

It seems to me that if the Jewish theory be true, these conclusions are correct, for they are in accord with this man's life, as is known and testified by both friends and foes, for the elements were no more in his hands than the clay in the hands of the potter. He could convert water into wine; he could change death into life, disease into health; he could calm the seas, still the storms, and call up fish with a silver coin in its mouth. Now, I say, if he could do all these things, which he did, and many more, as the Jews all testify, and it was doing these things that created this enmity against him—he was not charged with criminal offenses, nor was he charged with violating any law, nor of wronging any individual in person, and all these facts are known to thousands, as well by his foes as by his friends—I am almost ready to say, as did Manlius at the cross: "Truly this was the Son of God." Now noble Sovereign, this is as near the facts in the case as I can arrive at, and I have taken pains to make the statement very full, so that you may judge of my conduct upon the whole, as I hear that Antipater has said many hard things of me in this matter.

With the promise of faithfulness and good wishes to my noble Sovereign, I am your most obedient servant, Pontius Pilate."

ABOUT THE AUTHOR

As a teenager, Jack Manilla knew that he would not be stuck in a Western Pennsylvania factory town forever. Raised in a blue-collar family that inspired big dreams, Manilla worked to pay his college tuition and then rapidly climbed the ladder to corporate success, acquiring earthly possessions the American culture coveted: multiple homes, boats, cars, country club memberships and expensive furnishings. Fame, and fortune fed his ego.

Then in 1994 the American Dream became an agonizing nightmare when he made a decision that lost him everything. Financially shipwrecked by a storm on the saltwater sea of life, he washed ashore at Safety Harbor, Florida, living in an orange grove cracker bungalow.

After being humbled and broken during 18 months in "The Pink House," Manilla was ready to follow God unconditionally. He attained personal peace and professional success by integrating spiritual values and Biblical principles into his business and everyday life.